Microcomputer Systems

Microcomputer Systems

Ivan Flores

Computer Consultant
Professor of Computer Methodology
City University of New York

Christopher Terry

Systems Research and Development Division
Dun & Bradstreet

VNR

VAN NOSTRAND REINHOLD COMPANY
NEW YORK CINCINNATI TORONTO LONDON MELBOURNE

Library of Congress Catalog Card Number: 81-23980
ISBN: 0-442-26141-1

Manufactured in the United States of America

Published by Van Nostrand Reinhold Company Inc.
135 West 50th Street, New York, N.Y. 10020

Van Nostrand Reinhold Publishing
1410 Birchmount Road
Scarborough, Ontario MIP 2E7, Canada

Van Nostrand Reinhold Australia Pty. Ltd.
17 Queen Street
Mitcham, Victoria 3132, Australia

Van Nostrand Reinhold Company Limited
Molly Millars Lane
Wokingham, Berkshire, England

15 14 13 12 11 10 9 8 7 6 5 4 3 2 1

Library of Congress Cataloging in Publication Data

Flores, Ivan.
   Microcomputer systems.

   Includes index.
   1. Microcomputers.   I. Terry, Christopher.
II. Title.
QA76.5.F463   001.64   81-23980
ISBN 0-442-26141-1   AACR2

Preface

The importance of microprocessors and microcomputers is clear, if only from the evidence of the plethora of books on the subject. Assembly Language programming is enjoying a resurgence for this very reason. However, this "library" of books divides into two categories:

- Beginner's books for those who want to buy a computer or learn BASIC and do elementary things with their new acquisition.
- Technical books aimed at the engineer and OEM persons who design new products, which includes microprocessors.

There is a need for an intermediate book that fits between these two extremes. Whereas the microprocessor is just the processing part of the computer, and the microcomputer is a device capable of calculating without any input or output, the microcomputer system is an assemblage of equipment and software that is immediately able to do useful work. There are a large number of such turnkey systems on the market that can be put to immediate use. Systems can also be assembled by the potential user. It is much like the audio component market where we put together a tuner and an amplifier and a set of speakers. But it is more complicated than that because we cannot merely plug together computer components as you do audio components and expect them to work.

A microcomputer system consists of the following:

- The microcomputer, which includes a microprocessor, a memory, and other LSI components.

- Devices such as a console, keyboard, printer, and so forth.
- An operating system.
- Drivers and interfaces for the devices concerned.

This book is aimed at those with at least a beginner's skills and exposure to:

- Hardware — knowing how things are broken down into modules and circuit boards and connected together by cables and connectors.
- Software — knowing what a program is and does, and how one goes about getting it to solve your problem.
- Systems — knowing that the operating system is there to tie the program and hardware together to get your work done.
- Computer jargon — distinguishing bits from bytes and so forth, so as to make sense of specifications.
- Specifications — statements of the size, speed, capacity, timing, power requirements, and so forth for devices and hardware components.

Well, from this you can see that our audience excludes the extremes — the neophyte and the microcomputer engineer.

The book is divided into four parts. The first part is an introduction and a review of computer hardware and operating systems. The next two parts describe peripheral devices and the software that drives them and shows how these relate to the overall microcomputer system and its control program. The last part examines how the whole system fits together.

The first two chapters are introductory and review material with which the reader should be acquainted. The purpose is to establish a uniform terminology and to relate hardware and software.

Chapter 1 is devoted to hardware oriented toward the microcomputer system. Although the architecture of the small computer is not much different from the large computer, subsystem boundaries may be placed in somewhat different positions to reflect the physical organization of the subsystem on one or more circuit boards.

The central subsystem for the microcomputer is the microprocessor. As the name implies, it does the processing and contains the registers that store temporary results. The features of various micro-processors, including the number of registers, presence of a stack, command format, and addressability, are briefly reviewed.

The physical structure of the microcomputer is more important to the owner, perhaps, than that of a much larger mechanism. This is because a typical owner can purchase an additional memory board, for instance, for a few hundred dollars and expand the capacity of his computer immediately to suit his needs. Other changes are just as easy to make.

In considering the system, it is important to understand how the components are tied together. Two sections describe ports interfaces, buses, and how IO controllers are attached within the system. Data is transmitted either serially by bit, or in parallel by byte. Since the former is so important for the microcomputer, a thorough discussion is found in the first chapter.

Chapter 2 introduces software concepts. First, the general need for an operating system for any computer is described with emphasis up-on those functions most important in the micro world. In most cases the operating system takes over as soon as the user turns on the power. A number of things take place during this time, some in the hardware and some in the software. These are described. A most important feature for the casual user is how he and the computer talk to each other. The user speaks through the console keyboard, the computer replies through the console display. Section 2.3 provides a broad brush description of this interplay by examining the role of the hardware and the software in this conversation.

Finally, in section 2.4, the various other functions needed for a complete computer system are superficially described. These include translators, utilities, and language translators. Also, the drivers that activate the input and the output device are put into prospective.

Since chapter 15 is devoted to a typical operating system, CPM, and shows how it is integrated with the computer hardware, it should be clear that chapter 2 is just an overview.

In the next two parts, the main portion of the text is devoted to describing the many devices that may be attached to the microcom-puter in such detail that the reader clearly sees their principles of op-eration. No two chapters have exactly the same format. However, these are the general principles used in constructing these chapters and their probable sequence:

- The general purpose and function of the device is described to convey its need and use from the operator's point of view.
- The overall components of the device and how they fit together are described.
- Each individual component is examined separately to give the alternative for its design and the actions for each alternative.
- Now that the device is seen as a whole, we examine how the components within it interact.
- The device interacts with the microcomputer by means of a software driver that is now investigated.

The bulk of the book, which concerns devices and storage, is divided into two parts. The first of these, actually the second part of the book, is devoted to the devices that accept information from a human operator or present data to him in either a temporary form, such as a display, or a more permanent form, such as a printout. The main memory of the computer is small compared to auxiliary storage available external to the microprocessor. Hence, Part III is concerned with auxiliary storage where data can be stored in machine-readable form and accessed at high speed. As a consequence, this data is not directly consumable by the human.

To start Part II, chapter 3 describes keyboard entry devices. The explanation follows the sequence described above. The fourth chapter on display is similarly constructed. Chapter 5 is on terminals, meaning compound devices that provide both a keyboard and a display. Terminals vary according to the amount of computing and storage capacity that each contains. The simplest terminals contain little or no additional capacity and hence are called "dumb." "Smart" terminals are so named because they exercise a certain amount of judgment without involving the microcomputer itself. This is because a microprocessor and some memory is included. Interface and drivers differ according to how intelligent the terminal may be.

Hard copy output is very important across the board from the smallest to the largest computer. A single printer can cost anywhere from a few hundred dollars to half a million dollars. This area offers the greatest contrast. These devices may be divided into three categories: low speed, medium speed, and high speed. The high-speed printer is indeed expensive, fast, and accurate, and far beyond the range of this volume.

Chapter 6 introduces printers and discusses the low-speed printer. Here we encounter a contrast between the low-speed, low-cost printer and the low-speed, moderate-cost printer, which produces high-quality output. Chapter 7 describes medium-speed printers, their operation, and the trade-offs designed into them.

So far we have seen two kinds of output — temporary, on the display screen, and permanent, the printed output. Both of these are text oriented. Pictures and diagrams are worth many words. But they are more complicated to generate. Again we have two alternatives — temporary, on the screen, and permanent, as produced by a printer or plotter. Both constitute the content of chapter 8.

The third part of the book is devoted to storage. Not all the data created is for immediate consumption; it is put on an auxiliary medium. Even for printed or displayed material, it is highly desirable to keep a machine-readable copy readily available. External storage devices provide for this.

Chapter 9 introduces external storage. It distinguishes between serial and random access and between temporary and permanent medium deformation. It introduces some of the current media and mentions other obsolete media (punched paper tape) and those not ordinarily used by the microcomputer system (punch cards).

The most important storage media use magnetic material for holding information. Since magnetic recording principles are used extensively in the following three chapters, it is important to get a good foundation in magnetic recording principles. Chapter 10 is devoted entirely to this topic. After the magnetic properties of materials are examined, recording methods are looked into. First, it is seen how audio recording has been adapted to the microcomputer. Then the many digital recording techniques, which are providing higher and higher recording density while maintaining reliability, are examined.

Chapter 11 describes tape and cassette drives. These are prevalent on the smallest and least expensive microcomputer systems such as the TRS-80 and Apple computers.

By far the most important storage device is the disk drive. From the medium-priced microcomputer system on up to maxicomputers, we find floppy discs brought into play. Fixed-disk drives are coming on strong. It is important to get a solid understanding of these devices and how they work.

Large amounts of data can be stored on the disk consisting of many files. How do these files share the large amount of space available on the disk? How do we keep track of free space. How do we control and manage access to the files? Chapter 13 is devoted to the organization and management of data on the disk medium. It deals with data layout and organization, the cataloging of the data and files, the file management system, and the software to control it. Finally, the file manager must interface with the operating system.

Data generated in the microcomputer system may be consumed immediately, stored, or sent some place else. It is this last area that chapter 14 considers. Data in memory must be reformatted and reorganized to be sent over telephone lines to another user or computer. The signals used within the computer must be put into a form that telephone lines can accept. A software driver has to supervise these activities.

The last part of the book, chapter 15, examines an overall system including CPM to see how the hardware, the operating system, the files, the data, and the program all fit together.

Thanks are due to Arlene Abend for the fabulous cover design. We would also like to express our gratitude to the staff at VNR for their constant assistance and encouragement, especially Larry Hager, Joan Lilly, Alberta Gordon and Anne Dempsey.

Ivan Flores

Christopher Terry

Contents

I
INTRODUCTION

1
The Hardware of Microcomputer Systems

1.1 INTRODUCTION

The prefix "micro" in microcomputer means "very small." It should convey that the computer, and the system of which it is part, is inexpensive and occupies very little space. It says nothing about the power of the computer.

Computer historians point out that the first real general purpose computer was the ENIAC, developed over 30 years ago. That computer occupied the space of an average apartment and consumed more power than the average apartment building. It cost over a $1/2 million to build but was worth the price because it provided scientific computing capability that was otherwise totally unavailable.

Isn't it amazing that this same power for calculating and providing clerical manipulation is available to the average person today for less than $10,000, consumes less electricity than the average television set and occupies no more room?

There is a wide range of microcomputers available in the marketplace. At the low end are small computers such as the Radio Shack pocket computer, which has a keyboard and can be programmed to solve many problems yet cannot print, store much data nor display it in an efficient fashion. In the middle range are computers costing between $1,500 and $4,000 such as the Apple and TRS-80. They are built for intermittent service and yet can be put to use in a commercial environment for small-business applications. At the top end there are computers between $6,000 and $20,000, some of which can serve several users simultaneously. These higher-priced machines are truly rugged and can be used continually day after day and year after year.

What can you do with this little computer? We are sure that if you have made an investment in a book such as this, you are aware of the wide range of functions that the computer can perform. At the bottom end there is entertainment and computer-assisted learning; at the top end there is the full-blown system which can act as your bookkeeper and accountant to perform all the functions needed for small business.

The computer is a personal helper. It manages our checking accounts, keeps our memos, provides schedules for us and even keeps track of our inventory of records, books or whatever.

You can connect your computer to the telephone and subscribe to services which give you the news, a directory of entertainment and current events. These sources can send you up-to-date information about recipes, styles, airline schedules, restaurants and so forth. You can even use it for electronic mail to send messages to people with computers in other cities.

When you get to the middle and upper category, you find that microcomputers can be used as word processors, which perform as well as or better than some leading commercial products. Both authors of this book wrote all of the manuscript on two word-processing programs, Magic Wand and Word-Master, respectively. The entire book was edited and put together on a word processor. The glossary and index were prepared on a microcomputer using BASIC programs and several commercial products. Even the spelling was checked with MicroSpell on a microcomputer.

Moderate-size microcomputers today have inexpensive programs which can solve most of your accounting problems. For between $50 and $2,000 you can get programs to do your accounts receivable, accounts payable, inventory, payroll and other special functions which the nature of your business demands. There are overall programs for database management which can coordinate all your activities and make it possible to ask questions of a generalized nature and get back coherent answers.

What are these *devices* connected to the computer which we mentioned earlier? First there is the keyboard. By means of alphabetic, numeric and control keys you tell the computer what you want it to do and qualify all your requests. This way you talk to it.

To get information from the computer another device is necessary. The very basic device provided with the least-expensive computer is the single line display, used in the Radio Shack Pocket Computer. More flexibility is provided with a cathode ray tube display found in all moderate through expensive computers.

A printer is more or less a basic necessity. A minimum printer which provides a readable printout can be bought for $500. Letter-quality printers cost $2,000 to $3,000 and produce excellent and rapid typing. Some business applications in the high range use line printers which operate at a very high speed and moderate quality — but they cost as much as some complete middle-size computers; that is, $6,000 or more.

You can get along without external storage, but it is rather difficult. The modest computer provides a cassette reader to bring in programs and to hold data. These cost only $50 to $100, but they are slow and ponderous. Most moderate to expensive computers use floppy disks. Drives for such disks cost only a few hundred dollars and provide fast and easy access to large amounts of storage. Even so, they are not sufficient for the purposes of small businesses and large word processing users. The trend is to hard disks, which can store five million to hundreds of millions of characters. The price of such equipment is going down steadily and will be accessible to the average user within a couple of years.

Other input and output devices are becoming popular. One of the most useful of these is the modem, which allows us to hook the computer up to telephone lines. Then there are controllers which can hook into light dimmers, thermostats and other detectors around your house to control them and turn them on and off. For this purpose a computer should have access to a real-time calendar and clock to tell it when to activate and receive information from the devices. Then we can connect to sound. There are devices to interpret speech and to create speech as well as music.

The purpose of this book is to examine the more common devices, to describe how they are connected together and to the computer, and to explain how the programs work which drive the devices and talk to you.

There are many other books which describe where, what, which and why. We believe if you know *how*, it is easy to find the answers to the other questions.

1.2 THE MICROCOMPUTER SYSTEM

What is a computer system?

The overall computer system consists of a computer, a number of devices which bring in or take out data, an operating system and programs. This text is concerned with all of these. The computer itself is given less attention than the other three because there are so many other books which describe the computer. The main emphasis here is upon input and output (I/O) devices and how they are connected with the computer. The operating system operates these devices, so we examine the routines and the drivers which activate the devices as well as the control program. Finally, we examine programs and how they are constructed and used.

Now, what is the computer? It consists of a processor and control electronics, a memory, a power supply and controllers. Most of the computer is housed in a single cabinet. On it are connectors. Cables plug into these connectors. On the other end of the cables we find devices which receive or transmit data.

The Physical Computer

Figure 1.1 is a sketch of a typical computer chassis with the cabinet removed.

At the rear right is the power supply which produces the regulated low voltage associated with such equipment. The power is sent to a motherboard consisting of a thick printed circuit board with connectors on the upper side and printed conductors linking these connectors on the under side. These conductors form the bus.

A bus structure is common in microcomputer systems. Bus is an abbreviation of the Latin word "omnibus," meaning (in the public transport sense) "for everybody" or (in the electronics field) "for every device." A bus includes power and signal conductors to energize all parts of the computer and allow them to communicate with each other.

I/O connectors   Cinch connectors   Power supply
on PC boards   for external devices   Ventilation fan   components

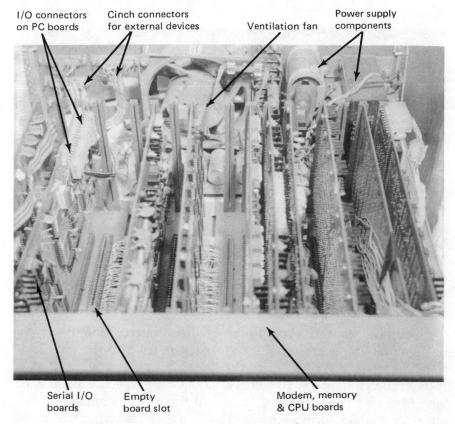

Serial I/O   Empty   Modem, memory
boards   board slot   & CPU boards

Figure 1.1.   Sketch of a typical microcomputer chassis.
(Courtesy of Tarbel Electronics, Inc.)

In the picture we see wires running from the motherboard to the front of the chassis. At intervals there are slot connectors into which printed circuit boards may be plugged. The number and type of these boards determines some of the characteristics of the computer, as we soon will see.

The connections to the outside world are through connectors at the back of the chassis. These are wired with ribbon cable to smaller connectors on the individual circuit boards. These boards contain circuits that match the bus to the external devices.

Oftentimes the diskette drive is included on the main chassis, but it may sometimes be housed separately and attached with a cable like the other devices.

Figure 1.2.   Typical circuit board for S-100 bus.

Figure 1.2 shows a typical printed circuit board. Boards vary in size from a few square inches to a few square feet; this example is of standard size for systems using the S-100 bus. It is a piece of glass epoxy (fiberglass) about 10 inches long, 5 inches high and about 1/16 inch thick. At the bottom of the board are printed a number of flat metal areas which form a connector. When the board is inserted in the slot, spring fingers make contact with these metal areas so that signals may pass between the board and the bus. Often the metallic areas are gold-plated to ensure good electrical contact.

Horizontal and vertical metal lines have been printed on both surfaces of the board and serve to conduct signals from one part of the board to another. Mounted on the board are a number of discrete components as well as sockets. The sockets are constructed to receive integrated circuit chips.

Microprocessor Board

The microprocessor board houses the central computer which does all the calculating and processing. The logical layout (the components) which constitute the subsystems and the way they are connected) is shown in Figure 1.3. At the center of the board is the microprocessor integrated circuit (IC). It consists of literally thousands of circuits. These include many registers to hold temporary data, commands, addresses and other things needed to keep the computing going. This is a single chip only a fraction of an inch in its largest dimension. It is put in a casing, and wires are brought out to prongs so that it may be inserted into an IC socket.

Although there is a tremendous amount of circuitry on this chip, other things are required in order to make a complete central processing unit (CPU). Some of these are named in the figure:

- A clock to provide timing signals.
- Amplifiers to make sure that signals are of proper amplitude.
- Switches which route the data.
- A panel driver to let an operator know what is happening.
- An interrupt circuit and handler to direct the computer's attention to priority activities.
- An auto jump circuit to bring in the operating system.

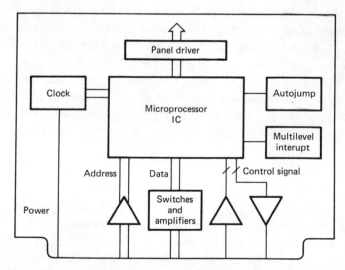

Figure 1.3. Logical layout of a micro/processor board.

The Microprocessor

Many companies have designed 8-bit microprocessor chips. The most important family of such chips includes the 8080 and 8085 from Intel and the Z80 from Zilog. These are compatible upward; that is, programs written for the 8080 run without change on the 8085 or Z80. They are listed in order of computing power. This family of 8-bit microprocessors is characterized by having several internal registers that can be used individually to store 8-bit numbers or in pairs to store 16-bit numbers.

The other important family includes the 6800 and 6809 from Motorola and the 6502 from MOS Technology. These have fewer registers for 8-bit numbers but additional 16-bit registers which provide memory addressing capabilities that the other family does not have.

Microprocessors in the 1980s will depend largely on the knowledge gained from experience with these chips.

All these microprocessors are described as 8-bit microprocessors. Their internal registers are 8 and 16 bits wide. Some can do 16-bit arithmetic, but their external data path and their connections to the bus are 8 bits wide. Memory addressing is for 8-bit words.

A new breed of microprocessor has become viable in the early 1980s. Chips which are 16 and even 32 bits wide are available. Microcomputers using these chips have appeared on the market, with operating systems to run them. There is no question that they will become less expensive and more powerful than their predecessors.

The design of the devices with which they interface is hardly affected by the components in the computers which use them. Hence, the user should not fear that the description of these devices in the rest of the book will be materially changed in the near future.

Memory

Memory space is generally reckoned in bytes or kilobytes (K). A byte is the smallest individually addressable memory unit and is a group of 8 bits. Because the numbers on which the computer operates are all powers of 2, a kilobyte is not 1,000 bytes, but 1,024 (2^{10}).

Directly addressable memory for a microcomputer system consists of up to 65,536 (64K) bytes for an 8-bit microprossor with

16 address lines, or 1,048,576 bytes for a 16-bit microprocessor with 20 address lines. Memory reference and branch instructions can access any location within this directly addressable space. An 8-bit machine using the S-100 bus (which has 20 address lines) can have up to 16 banks of 64K each (over 1 megabyte in all) but can address only one bank at a time. Selection of a particular bank requires a 4-bit hardware register on the board into which the four most significant address bits are loaded by a separate output instruction. This register is addressed as an I/O port.

Another way to switch memory banks is to put the register and its support circuitry on a separate memory management circuit board which plugs into the bus. Either arrangement is used in multiuser systems, where a separate bank may be assigned to each user.

The memory elements are large scale integration LSI chips of three types:

- Random access (read/write) memory (RAM)
- Read-only memory (ROM)
- Programmable read-only memory (PROM)

Read/Write Memory (RAM).   RAM chips are provided with address lines, the number depending on how the internal storage is organized. For example, a chip that stores 4,096 (4K) bits may be organized as 4,096 1-bit cells, in which case it has 12 address lines; or it may be organized as 1,024 4-bit cells, in which case it has 10 address lines. Common chip sizes are $1K \times 1$, $1K \times 4$, $4K \times 1$ and $16K \times 1$ for RAM; and 32×8, 256×8, 512×8, $1K \times 8$ and $2K \times 8$ for ROM. In addition to address inputs, which are connected via buffers to the corresponding low-order address lines on the bus, memory chips also have one or more chip select inputs which are enabled by signals decoded from the high-order address bus lines.

For example, a memory board with storage for $4K \times 8$ might consist of four rows of eight $1K \times 1$ memory chips. The four most significant bus address lines are decoded to generate a board enable signal; switches allow the user to determine which 4K segment of the total memory space the board will occupy. The next two bus address lines are decoded on the board to provide four row enable signals. All the chips in one row have their chip select inputs connected to the

corresponding row enable signal. The 10 least significant address bus lines are connected to the 10 address inputs on each chip through buffers.

The 8-bit microprocessors read or write 8 bits at a time; if a 16-bit number is to be read or written, this is done in two stages. Some memory reference instructions access 1 byte only; others access 2 bytes but require more clock cycles to do so. The 16-bit microprocessors generally use memory that is 16 bits wide, but also have the ability to access either half of a 16-bit memory cell.

RAM memory may be static or dynamic. Static memory stores the data in transistor circuits. Once data has been written into an address, it is held there as long as power is on. It is overwritten by new data. Dynamic memory stores each data bit as an electric charge on a solid-state capacitor; the charge dissipates with time and must be refreshed every few milliseconds. Static memory consumes more power because its action depends on current through transistors rather than static charges on the solid-state capacitors contained in static memory. Dynamic memory is somewhat cheaper than static; it is widely used in systems where low cost is important and where the refreshing mechanism does not interfere with the operation of other components of the system.

Read-Only Memory (ROM).   ROM memory chips are manufactured with data permanently written in each memory location. When an address is placed on the address lines by the microprocessor (and the ROM chip is enabled), the memory places the data on the data bus. It is not possible to write data into a ROM chip. ROM is used for holding programs such as monitors, BASIC interpreters or control programs. When you turn the power on, the microcomputer executes a jump to the starting location of the program in ROM and starts executing it.

ROM is suitable for mass production of small computer systems; the design of the program and masks for the memory chips are expensive, but since thousands of copies of the ROM are made the copies are inexpensive. Inexpensive ROMs holding large programs that do not disappear when power is turned off make possible the production of inexpensive home computers such as the Radio Shack TRS-80, Atari, Commodor PET and others.

Programmable Read-Only Memory (PROM).   PROM is read-only memory which can be programmed by the user. It is supplied as a blank chip containing 1s in every location. To program a particular location in the PROM, place the desired address on the address lines and the desired bit pattern on the data lines and then apply a "programming voltage." At the addressed location, the 1 bits are unaffected; for the 0 bits, the programming voltage burns out a fusible link (in the same way that a short circuit blows a house fuse).

Small PROMs organized as 32 8-bit words (type 82S23) are permanently changed when the programming is performed; the data burned into them cannot be erased. Larger PROM chips, organized as 256, 512, 1,024 or 2,048 8-bit words (types 1702, 6834, 2708 or 2716) are programmed differently; they are erasable by the user. A quartz window allows the chip to be exposed to high-intensity ultraviolet light; an exposure of about 15 minutes erases all data previously programmed into the chip. The fusible links are not metal (as in the 82S23) but a conductive crystalline substance which flows under the action of ultraviolet light and bridges the gaps previously created by the programming. These EPROMs (erasable programmable read-only memory) can be erased and reprogrammed several hundred times, although erasure time increases toward the end of the useful life of the chip.

EPROMs let you create nonvolatile but modifiable programs such as bootstraps, input-output routines or complete operating systems. The user is in no way dependent on the manufacturer for the end result, whereas ROM programs can be created only by the chip manufacturer, since the programming is an integral part of the manufacturing process.

Interconnection

Figure 1.4 shows the interconnection of the components on the microcomputer chassis. At the top we see the power supply and the motherboard described earlier. The latter provides connectors for cables to external devices.

The bus wires from the motherboard go to slots (connectors). One of these certainly houses the microprocessor board (any one). Next, we must provide for memory. Most of it is probably random access

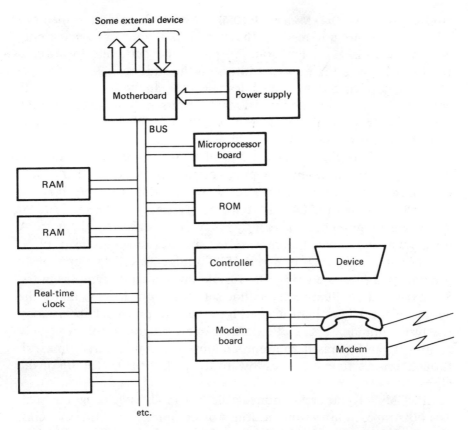

Figure 1.4. Interconnection of components on microcomputer chassis.

memory (RAM) from which we can read or write. With the current technology, single boards provide as much as 65,536 (64K) bytes (8-bit words). Boards with as little as 8K can be purchased. Most microprocessors can directly address up to 64K. However, an additional board costs money, so it is up to the user to decide how much memory he needs.

The newest boards allow for bank switching. This allows several different banks of memory (each containing up to 64K) to be addressed by a microprocessor that has only 16 address pins, provided that the bus has the four extra lines required for bank selection.

Read-only memory (ROM) is useful for important programs and the operating system. Since its contents are not destroyed when the machine is turned off, the user is assured of the availability of the operating system when power is switched on again.

Other slots on the bus may be used for such hardware components as:

- The controller for one or more disk drives.
- A modem board to hook into the telephone line and thence to the large computer system.
- A real-time calendar and clock.
- Analog interfaces to thermostats, lighting, etc.
- Pattern generators for graphics.
- Music synthesizers.

1.3 BUSES

Many microcomputers are built around a bus structure. In some hardwired computers, there are wires dedicated to communication between the CPU and the memory, and other wires dedicated to communication between the CPU and a communications interface, and yet other wires dedicated to communication between the CPU and a printer controller. With a bus, an assemblage of wires or conducting strips on a printed circuit board, communication between different parts of the system takes place over a fixed set of common conductors that are routed to all circuit board sockets within the computer. The bus consists of several groups of wires, each serving a distinct function. We name these as follows:

- *Power* lines distribute voltage and current to all subsystems.
- *Address* lines select a memory location or I/O controller.
- *Data* lines carry a specified number of data bits, usually 8, 16, or 32.
- *Control* lines pass timing and initiating signals form one subsystem to another. In this category we have, for instance:
  - Timing signals.
  - Memory commands.
  - I/O requests.
  - Interrupt request and acknowledge.
  - Wait and idle signals.

Sometimes these groups of wires are also called a bus—we speak of an "address bus," a "data bus," etc.

A simplified diagram of a bus connecting different sections of a computer is shown in Figure 1.5. Figure 1.6 shows some of the components of a typical microcomputer plugged into their motherboard, and Figure 1.7 shows the underside of the motherboard with the 100 printed-circuit traces of the standard S-100 bus.

Why Use a Bus?   All the current bus structures have been designed with two goals in view:

1. Standardization of the mechanical characteristics of major components of the computer system, with the concomitant reduction in manufacturing costs.
2. Flexibility in system configuration.

Although the manufacturing cost of each circuit board may be slightly increased by designing it to conform to the connector pattern, the cost of connecting boards into the system is reduced. The printed-circuit motherboard is mass-produced at a price well below that of a cable harness. Any number of additional circuit boards of different types can later be incorporated into the system as needed, merely by plugging them into the standard bus and providing suitable software drivers. This flexibility allows a manufacturer to create a whole family

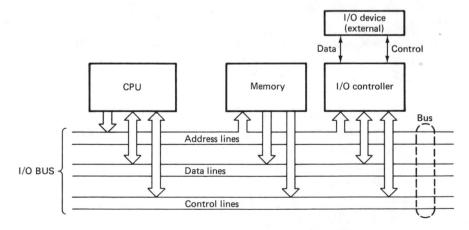

Figure 1.5. Typical bus system; simplified block diagram.

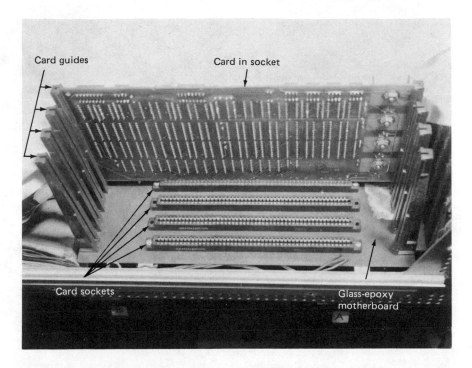

Figure 1.6.   Circuit boards plugged into a motherboard.

of computer systems, with more or fewer slots, suited to different classes of users.

Characteristics of the Available Buses.   There is no universally adopted bus structure; nor could there possibly be one that suited all microcomputer architectures on the market. Several bus structures that are in common use are now examined.

Microcomputer Buses.   An 8-bit microprocessor is one which manipulates addresses and data in 8-bit bytes. For 8-bit microcomputers, there are three popular buses:

- The S-50 bus for microcomputers based on the 6800 chip.
- The S-100 bus, originated by MITS, Inc. for their altair 8080-based microcomputer.
- Intel's Multibus, used in all development and industrial systems manufactured by Intel.

Figure 1.7. Underside of motherboard.

Although the S-100 bus has weaknesses such as some undefined lines and the need for support circuitry to generate some of the control signals, it is more flexible because every connector on the motherboard receives all the bus lines. Thus, any board can be plugged into any slot. This is not true of the S-50 bus, where slots are associated with specific groups of memory addresses. An Institute of Electrical and Electronic Engineers (IEEE) standard is in progress for the S-100 bus; many boards are already built to conform to the preliminary specifications. It can accommodate many microprocessors. There are S-100 CPU boards on the market for numerous 8-bit processor chips (8080, 8085, Z-80, 2650, F8, 6502, 6800, 6802 and 6809) and five 16-bit CPU boards (8086, 9900, LSI-11, Z-8000 and Pascal Microengine), all conforming to the provisional IEEE standard/696.

The S-100 bus provides 24 address lines, allowing direct addressing of up to 16 megabytes of memory, and supports bank-switching of memory blocks.

The 16 data lines can be used as 8 data in and 8 data out for 8-bit CPUs, or as a 16-bit bidirectional data bus for 16-bit CPUs.

Pin assignments for the S-100 bus are shown in Table 1-1.

External Buses.   An external bus provides a standard set of lines and a standard pin configuration to exchange data with external devices hooked to it. For example, there is the IEEE-488 bus to hook up with instruments and analog devices. It is becoming of greater importance each year as more instrument manufacturers provide IEEE-488 interfacing circuitry in their products.

Two other external buses are the Electronic Industries Association (EIA) standards RS-232C and RS-449. These connect the computer to devices that provide serial communications over private, leased or switched public telephone lines.

Internal Bus Design.   Besides the description of sets of wires and their pin configuration, a bus standard specifies the upper and lower limits of the electrical signals carried by each bus group. Each type of computer has address and data lines, and the timing and sequence of control signals is rigidly maintained to ensure the rapid transfer of valid data from one part of the system to another. Where clock frequencies of 2 megahertz and up are involved, the electrical characteristics of the bus lines themselves have a large influence in the reliable operation of the system. Every conductor has a characteristic inductance and capacitance with respect to the other conductors. The signals dealt with by the computer are on-off. Voltage or current is switched on or off suddenly, thereby creating steep wavefronts. The frequency at which these changes occur is the *clock rate*. The signals are *not* sinusoidal but are square waves with sharp rise and fall time. Harmonics, up to the tenth, of significant size are present, and must be transmitted for reliable switching. For a clock rate of 2 MHz, the bus must transmit 20 MHz with low loss.

The physical layout of the bus is of importance. Inductance and capacitance are determined by the spacing between wires, components, connectors and the chassis, as well as by the shape and length of the path. A well-designed bus isolates critical signal lines from others or interposes ground lines.

Table 1-1 S-100 bus pin list.

PIN NO.	SIGNAL & TYPE	ACTIVE LEVEL		DESCRIPTION
1	+ 8 VOLTS (B)			Instantaneous minimum greater than 7 volts, instantaneous maximum less than 25 volts, average maximum less than 11 volts.
2	+ 16 VOLTS (B)			Instantaneous minimum greater than 14.5 volts, instantaneous maximum less than 35 volts, average maximum less than 21.5 volts.
3	XRDY (S)	H		One of two ready inputs to the current bus master. The bus is ready when both these ready inputs are true. See pin 72.
4	VI0* (S)	L	O.C.	Vectored interrupt line 0.
5	VI1* (S)	L	O.C.	Vectored interrupt line 1.
6	VI2* (S)	L	O.C.	Vectored interrupt line 2.
7	VI3* (S)	L	O.C.	Vectored interrupt line 3.
8	VI4* (S)	L	O.C.	Vectored interrupt line 4.
9	VI5* (S)	L	O.C.	Vectored interrupt line 5.
10	VI6* (S)	L	O.C.	Vectored interrupt line 6.
11	VI7* (S)	L	O.C.	Vectored interrupt line 7.
12	NMI* (S)	L	O.C.	Non-maskable interrupt.
13	PWRFAIL* (B)	L		Power fail bus signal. (See Section 2.10.1 regarding pseudo open-collector nature)
14	DMA3* (M)	L	O.C.	Temporary master priority bit 3.
15	A18 (M)	H		Extended address bit 18.
16	A16 (M)	H		Extended address bit 16.
17	A17 (M)	H		Extended address bit 17.
18	SDSB* (M)	L	O.C.	The control signal to disable the 8 status signals.
19	CDSB* (M)	L	O.C.	The control signal to disable the 5 control output signals.
20	GND (B)			Common with pin 100.
21	NDEF			Not to be defined. Manufacturer must specify any use in detail.
22	ADSB* (M)	L	O.C.	The control signal to disable the 16 address signals.
23	DODSB* (M)	L	O.C.	The control signal to disable the 8 data output signals.
24	ϕ (B)	H		The master timing signal for the bus.
25	pSTVAL* (M)	L		Status valid strobe.
26	pHLDA (M)	H		A control signal used in conjunction with HOLD* to coordinate bus master transfer operations.
27	RFU			Reserved for future use.
28	RFU			Reserved for future use.
29	A5 (M)	H		Address bit 5.
30	A4 (M)	H		Address bit 4.
31	A3 (M)	H		Address bit 3.
32	A15 (M)	H		Address bit 15 (most significant for non-extended addressing).
33	A12 (M)	H		Address bit 12

Table 1-1 (Continued)

PIN NO.	SIGNAL & TYPE	ACTIVE LEVEL		DESCRIPTION
34	A9 (M)	H		Address bit 9.
35	DO1 (M)/DATA1 (M/S)	H		Data out bit 1, bidirectional data bit 1.
36	DO0 (M)/DATA0 (M/S)	H		Data out bit 0, bidirectional data bit 0.
37	A10 (M)	H		Address bit 10.
38	DO4 (M)/DATA4 (M/S)	H		Data out bit 4, bidirectional data bit 4.
39	DO5 (M)/DATA5 (M/S)	H		Data out bit 5, bidirectional data bit 5.
40	DO6 (M)/DATA6 (M/S)	H		Data out bit 6, bidirectional data bit 6.
41	DI2 (S)/DATA10 (M/S)	H		Data in bit 2, bidirectional data bit 10.
42	DI3 (S)/DATA11 (M/S)	H		Data in bit 3, bidirectional data bit 11.
43	DI7 (S)/DATA15 (M/S)	H		Data in bit 7, bidirectional data bit 15.
44	sM1 (M)	H		The status signal which indicates that the current cycle is an op-code fetch.
45	sOUT (M)	H		The status signal identifying the data transfer bus cycle to an output device.
46	sINP (M)	H		The status signal identifying the data transfer bus cycle from an input device.
47	sMEMR (M)	H		The status signal identifying bus cycles which transfer data from memory to a bus master, which are not interrupt acknowledge instruction fetch cycle(s).
48	sHLTA (M)	H		The status signal which acknowledges that a HLT instruction has been executed.
49	CLOCK(B)			2 MHz (0.5%) 40-60% duty cycle. Not required to be synchronous with any other bus signal.
50	GND (B)			Common with pin 100.
51	+ 8 VOLTS (B)			Common with pin 1.
52	− 16 VOLTS (B)			Instantaneous maximum less than −14.5 volts, instantaneous minimum greater than −35 volts, average minimum greater than −21.5 volts.
53	GND (B)			Common with pin 100.
54	SLAVE CLR* (B)	L	O.C.	A reset signal to reset bus slaves. Must be active with POC* and may also be generated by external means.
55	DMA0* (M)	L	O.C.	Temporary master priority bit 0.
56	DMA1* (M)	L	O.C.	Temporary master priority bit 1.
57	DMA2* (M)	L	O.C.	Temporary master priority bit 2.
58	sXTRQ* (M)	L		The status signal which requests 16-bit slaves to assert SIXTN*.
59	A19 (M)	H		Extended address bit 19.
60	SIXTN* (S)	L	O.C.	The signal generated by 16-bit slaves in response to the 16-bit request signal sXTRQ*.
61	A20 (M)	H		Extended address bit 20.
62	A21 (M)	H		Extended address bit 21.
63	A22 (M)	H		Extended address bit 22.
64	A23 (M)	H		Extended address bit 23.
65	NDEF			Not to be defined signal.
66	NDEF			Not to be defined signal.

Table 1-1 (Continued)

PIN NO.	SIGNAL & TYPE	ACTIVE LEVEL		DESCRIPTION
67	PHANTOM* (M/S)	L	O.C.	A bus signal which disables normal slave devices and enables phantom slaves–primarily used for bootstrapping systems without hardware front panels.
68	MWRT (B)	H		pWR•–sOUT (logic equation). This signal must follow pWR* by not more than 30 ns. (See note, Section 2.7.5.3)
69	RFU			Reserved for future use.
70	GND (B)			Common with pin 100.
71	RFU			Reserved for future use.
72	RDY (S)	H	O.C.	See comments for pin 3.
73	INT* (S)	L	O.C.	The primary interrupt request bus signal.
74	HOLD* (M)	L	O.C.	The control signal used in conjuction with pHLDA to coordinate bus master transfer operations.
75	RESET* (B)	L	O.C.	The reset signal to reset bus master devices. This signal must be active with POC* and may also be generated by external means.
76	pSYNC (M)	H		The control signal identifying BS_1.
77	pWR* (M)	L		The control signal signfying the presence of valid data on DO bus or data bus.
78	pDBIN (M)	H		The control signal that requests data on the DI bus or data bus from the currently addressed slave.
79	A0 (M)	H		Address bit 0 (least signficant).
80	A1 (M)	H		Address bit 1.
81	A2 (M)	H		Address bit 2.
82	A6 (M)	H		Address bit 6.
83	A7 (M)	H		Address bit 7.
84	A8 (M)	H		Address bit 8.
85	A13 (M)	H		Address bit 13.
86	A14 (M)	H		Address bit 14.
87	A11 (M)	H		Address bit 11.
88	DO2 (M)/DATA2 (M/S)	H		Data out bit 2, bidirectional data bit 2.
89	DO3 (M)/DATA3 (M/S)	H		Data out bit 3, bidirectional data bit 3.
90	DO7 (M)/DATA7 (M/S)	H		Data out bit 7, bidirectional data bit 7.
91	DI4 (S)/DATA12 (M/S)	H		Data in bit 4 and bidirectional data bit 12.
92	DI5 (S)/DATA13 (M/S)	H		Data in bit 5 and bidirectional data bit 13.
93	DI6 (S)/DATA14 (M/S)	H		Data in bit 6 and bidirectional data bit 14.
94	DI1 (S)/DATA9 (M/S)	H		Data in bit 1 and bidirectional data bit 9.
95	DI0 (S)/DATA8 (M/S)	H		Data in bit 0 (least signficant for 8-bit data) and bidirectional data bit 8.
96	sINTA (M)	H		The status signal identifying the bus input cycle(s) that may follow an accepted interrupt request presented on INT*.
97	sWO* (M)	L		The status signal identifying a bus cycle which transfers data from a bus master to a slave.
98	ERROR* (S)	L	O.C.	The bus status signal signifying an error condition during present bus cycle.
99	POC* (B)	L		The power-on clear signal for all bus devices; when this signal goes low, it must stay low for at least 10 msecs.
100	GND (B)			System ground.

Small connector size is desirable for decreasing the bulk of the equipment. But it constrains the design: very narrow conductors are fragile and subject to unwanted leakage via metallic dust from the environment or from manufacturing mishaps.

1.4 INTERFACES

Peripherals are relatively slow; they are designed to be located at a distance from the CPU. Timing and voltage levels may be quite different from those produced or expected by the computer. Hence, communication between the CPU and a peripheral takes place through an *interface*. Two distinct interface circuits are needed: the CPU side and the device side. The CPU side responds to CPU signals presented on the bus and generates suitable acknowledgements at information rates and signal levels compatible with the CPU. The device side transfers data and control signals to and from the peripheral at information rates and signal levels compatible with the peripheral. A separate interface is provided for each peripheral connected to the computer. On the CPU side, these interfaces are all similar. On the device side, interfaces vary according to the type of peripheral.

A block diagram of a typical interface is shown in Figure 1.8. The CPU side performs the following functions:

- Decodes and responds to the unique address from the CPU that identifies the associated peripheral device.
- Decodes and responds to CPU control signals indicating the direction of the data transfer to be performed.
- Waits for the CPU to request a data transfer and
  (1) Transfers commands or output data from the data bus to an output register.
  (2) Transfers device status or input data from an input register to the data bus
- May generate an interrupt request signal when the peripheral is ready to perform a data transfer in either direction.

Above, and in later discussion, the CPU is considered the referent for direction of transfer: *output* is from the CPU to the peripheral; *input* is from the peripheral to the CPU. It is important to remember this

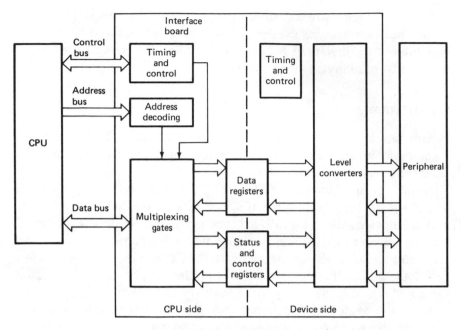

Figure 1.8. Typical CPU/peripheral interface; block diagram.

when considering interfaces and communication devices, which face both ways.

A peripheral is either an input device (sending to the CPU) or an output device (receiving from the CPU), not both. A bidirectional peripheral such as a terminal, modem or magnetic tape unit is labeled as though it consisted of two devices, one for input and the other for output. Its interface contains separate data transfer and command/status circuits for each direction. The two "devices" are kept functionally distinct, both from the hardware and the programming points of view, even when the input and output interfaces are on the same circuit board and share one addressing logic.

The device side of the interface shown in Figure 1.8 performs the following functions:

- Converts all signals from the voltage levels used in the computer to RS-232 (or other) levels used by the peripheral, and vice versa.

- Interrogates the device to determine the busy/ready status of various functions, and sets or resets corresponding bits in its status register, which is accessible to the CPU.
- Notifies an output device that data is ready in the output register; may wait for acknowledgement before sending a data strobe to perform the transfer, but the data ready signal is sometimes also used as the strobe.
- Performs input and error detection (parity), and sets or resets corresponding bits in the status register.

1.5 I/0 ADDRESSING

Two types of I/O addressing mechanism are common in microcomputers:

- Port I/O.
- Memory-mapped I/O.

Port I/O

For port I/O there are at least two CPU machine language commands, one for input, the other for output. Each command consists of an operation code and a port address. Decoding and executing the command

1. Places this address on the address bus.
2. Puts signals on the control bus which identify the operation as I/O, not memory, and specify the direction of transfer.

A datum is transferred between a CPU register and a register in the interface, via the data bus.

Memory-Mapped I/O

A memory-mapped I/O operation is executed like a memory read or write operation. The datum is transferred from any CPU register to a memory address. However, no memory exists at that address; instead, that location is decoded as an I/O interface. This method is used by CPUs (such as the 6800 microprocessor) which do not have separate input or output instructions in their repertoire.

Memory-mapped I/O has the advantage that any convenient CPU register can be used for data transfers (port I/O always uses the A register). This can sometimes eliminate a transfer into the A register. Indeed, different sections of a program may use different CPU registers for I/O. Further, the whole set of memory reference instructions is applicable to I/O. For example, the 8080 and Z80 increment/decrement register instructions treat memory as a register and modify the content of the location pointed to by the address register pair. Hence, these fast 1-byte instructions can also modify an I/O device register (port I/O needs several 2-byte instructions to do this).

A disadvantage is that memory addresses used for I/O operations cannot also address real memory. This is bad enough, but since memory is typically addressable only in 4K blocks, use of even one address for I/O renders the entire 4K block of addresses unavailable for RAM. In dedicated controller applications where programs are usually small, this may be of no consequence. However, when microcomputers run FORTRAN, COBOL, or Pascal compilers, which require large blocks of memory as well as resident operating systems, the loss of 4K may be serious.

Program-Driven or Interrupt-Driven I/O?

I/O operations can further be classified as:

- Program-driven: the main program determines when I/O devices are to be serviced.
- Polled I/O: the main program regularly interrogates each device in turn to see if it requires service.
- Interrupt-driven: the main program does not give time to I/O devices until one of them signals that it is ready to output a character or has a character ready in its buffer.

We now discuss how these methods work.

I/O Drivers. A *driver* is a software routine that accomplishes data transfers between the CPU and a specific peripheral device having a unique I/O address.

Program-Driven I/O. Program-driven (or simply, programmed) I/O is widely used in small, single-user microcomputer systems because it is simple. Its main characteristic is that for each transfer the CPU waits in a loop until the peripheral is ready. To print a line of text from a work area, the print routine places a character in a register and calls a printer driver subroutine which does the following:

1. Saves the character in another register or on the stack.
2. Interrogates the printer interface status register repeatedly until the ready bit goes true.
3. Restores the character to the source register.
4. Transfers the character to the printer interface.
5. Returns control to the calling routine.

Figure 1.9 illustrates this process in a flowchart. The print routine continues calling the driver subroutine until all characters have been transferred to the printer.

For a transfer rate of 300 bits per second over a serial line, the time required to empty the interface serial output register is 3.3 milliseconds, whereas the CPU takes only a few microseconds to get another character from memory. Thus, the CPU may spend over 90 percent of its time waiting in this loop and unavailable for other processing.

Polled I/O. It may be asked, "Could the CPU be applied to other work and return after an interval to examine the I/O busy flag?" This kind of operation is often found in minicomputer programs with minicomputer instructions that have the same word length and execute in the same time. Microprocessor instructions, on the contrary, may be 1, 2, 3 or 4 bytes long, and even instructions of the same length may require a different number of clock cycles to complete. When it is necessary to keep the printer running at top speed, the timing calculations are too horrendous to be worthwhile. An interrupt structure, described below, is a far more economical solution.

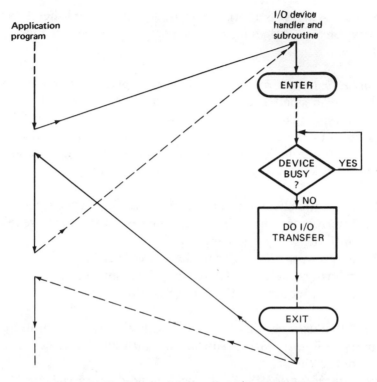

Figure 1.9.   Program-Controlled I/O, Flow Chart.

However, when two slow devices, such as a manual keyboard and a 300 bit per second communications line are working together, polled I/O is sometimes used. Here the keyboard status and the input line status are alternately examined. If either device has a character ready, it is processed, but such processing has to be simple, otherwise data may be lost. Figure 1.10 shows a flowchart of a routine performing polled I/O in this fashion.

Interrupt-Driven I/O. An interrupt structure ensures that the CPU gives time to I/O devices only when they call for attention. After an I/O transfer has occurred, for instance, the CPU is free to perform other operations without checking I/O status flags. When an I/O device becomes ready to send or accept data, it not only sets a "ready" flag accessible to the program, but also presents the "ready" status on an interrupt request line in the control bus. The CPU completes

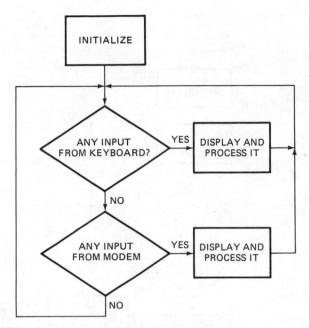

Figure 1.10.   Polled I/O flow chart.

the current instruction and inhibits further interrupt requests. Then the program stores the CPU state (i.e., the contents of all CPU registers and condition flags) on the stack and branches to a routine that identifies the interrupting device and performs the I/O operation required. Upon conclusion of the data transfer to (or from) the I/O device, the CPU registers (including the program counter) are restored from the stock, and the interrupted program picks up where it left off. Thus the time that under a programmed I/O scheme was spent waiting in loops can now be utilized for computation or for servicing other I/O devices. The process is illustrated in Figure 1.11.

If the CPU has only a single interrupt request line, the interrupt request causes a branch to a fixed location in memory where a general service routine is located. The service routine then checks each I/O device's status register. A flag there, when set, indicates that the associated device requested service. This polling process may require a number of instructions, particularly if there are many I/O devices. To reduce the overhead, many microprocessors provide for "vectored interrupts."

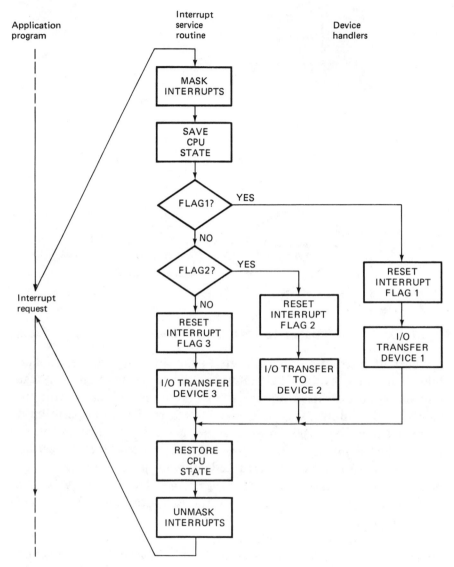

Figure 1.11. Polled interrupts flow chart.

Vectored Interrupts. For an 8080-based CPU, as an example, the vectored interrupt structure requires only a single interrupt request line. When the request is acknowledged by the CPU, the interrupting device places a byte on the data bus. In the 8080, this byte is treated as a value in the range 0 through 7 representing a subroutine call to one of eight reserved locations at octal addresses 000, 010, 020, 030, 040, 050, 060 and 070, respectively. The Z80 can use this interrupt mode, but is has another mode in which the byte is treaded as the low-order half of the address of a reserved location; there may be up to 128 of these located anywhere in memory. Each interrupting device is assigned to one of these reserved locations, at which there is a jump instruction to the device service routine. For the 8080 vectored interrupt scheme, a support chip called a priority encoder effectively divides the CPU interrupt request line into eight subsidiary request lines available to the I/O devices. If more than eight devices are connected, each of the subsidiary interrupt lines can be further multiplexed; identification of a multiplexed interrupting device then becomes the responsibility of the service routine.

The Z80 has other interrupt modes, and other microprocessors have interrupt structures which work differently in detail but nevertheless also allow an interrupting device to be identified by the hardware so that time is not lost by polling each device in turn.

An output device that is ready to accept data sets a ready bit in the interface status register to request an interrupt. To avoid frequent interrupts from devices that are ready but are not currently being used by the program, it is customary to allow these devices to be *masked*. Masks (bits in the program status register) are set by the service routine to prevent a device from making an interrupt. This is particularly important when a service routine is storing the state of the interrupted program on the stack. If further interrupts were to take place during this time, the storing action would be disrupted, and it would be impossible to get back to the application program that was suspended by the first request.

Nonmaskable Interrupt (NMI). There are also occasions when an interrupt request may cause the CPU to execute a halt instruction. If all interrupts were then disabled, the CPU could not be restarted without powering down. Some microprocessors are therefore provided with a nonmaskable interrupt request line which can always be activated either by the manual reset switch or by a real-time clock after a certain time interval. This facility ensures that the CPU can always be restarted without turning off power first.

Daisy Chain NMI.   A number of microprocessors, such as the Intel 8085 and Zilog Z-8000, allow more than one device to use the nonmaskable interrupt. They provide an interrupt enable line in the control bus to which each peripheral controller is connected in a daisy chain, as shown in Figure 1.12. The interrupt request output of each controller is connected to the nonmaskable interrupt (NMI) line via a gate that is armed by the interrupt enable.

A controller may generate an interrupt request only when its IEI (interrupt enable in) terminal is high. To generate an interrupt request, the controller pulls down the NMI request line and its IEO (interrupt enable out) terminal. Controllers further down the interrupt enable line are therefore inhibited from requesting service; however, controllers which have higher priority and are nearer to the +5-volt source of interrupt enable are allowed to interrupt service of the device that made the original request, if the interrupt system is enabled.

Priority is allocated to devices on the basis of speed, for both the priority encoder and the daisy chain interrupt enable. A typewriter terminal operating at 30 characters (300 bits) per second calls for service approximately every 3 milliseconds. Once the CPU has accepted a character, there is a 3-millisecond interval available to the CPU before the next character might be sent. However, for a CRT terminal operating at 960 characters (9,600 bits) per second, the interval is only about 100 microseconds. If the CPU does not service the CRT terminal within that time, data is lost. Therefore, the faster device is always allocated a higher priority in the interrupt chain.

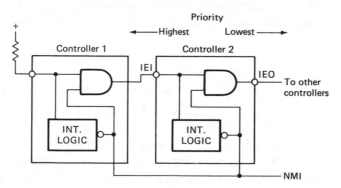

Figure 1.12.   Daisy-chain interrupt scheme; simplified logic.

Nested Interrupts.   For multiple interrups, shown in Figure 1.13, the main program is interrupted by device 3 (a slow device). All other interrupts are inhibited during the time that the application program status is being saved. Once this has been done, the interrupts are enabled again. During the course of servicing device 3, an interrupt request is received from device 1 (highest priority); this request is immediately honored, and the status of the service routine for device 3 is saved.

Near the end of the routine servicing device 1, an interrupt request is received from device 2. Since this device has lower priority than the device currently being serviced, the request is held off. When the service routine for device 1 is done, waiting interrupts are enabled. The request of device 2 is now being honored, since it has a higher priority than device 3, whole service remains suspended. Upon completion of the service for device 2, control passes back to the routine for the device which made the first request, and only when that has been satisfied does control revert to the application program.

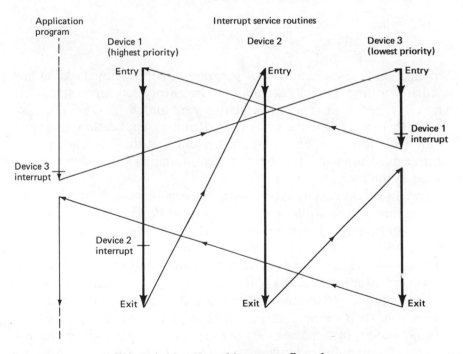

Figure 1.13.   Nested interrupts flow chart.

2
Softwear Concepts

2.1 SYSTEM SOFTWARE

Like its larger relatives the minicomputer and the maxicomputer, the microcomputer can do no useful work until it is provided with programs of two types:

- Application software.
- System software.

Application software consists of programs that perform tasks of immediate utility—payroll accounting, inventory control, statistical analysis of data, or games in which players match their skill against each other or against the computer. Running application programs is the real business of any computer system, but their development is outside the scope of this book. The requirements are as many and as varied as the users.

System software, however, is our concern because it provides the programming tools without which an application programmer would be almost helpless. It is possible (though tricky) to write a short program in machine language, entering it manually into memory through address and data switches provided on some computer front panels. However, entering more than 50 or so bytes in this manner is tedious and error-prone. If the front panel has only a power switch and a reset button, then we need an operating system even to type machine language codes into memory via the keyboard. Some systems have a *monitor* program in read-only memory to do this. Other systems have a small *bootstrap* loader program in read-only memory to load an operating system from cassette or disk.

The operating system is the primary system software component, without which we can do nothing of importance; the other components are programming aids that facilitate the creation and execution of large and complex application programs. We distinguish the following kinds of system software:

- The operating system (OS), which handles all input/output (I/O) and file management operations.
- Utility programs, including:
  - Text editors, to create and modify text files (such as the file for this book) or program files in assembly language or a high-level language.
  - Assemblers, to convert assembly language source files to executable machine code.
  - Print programs to print text files or hexadecimal representations of executable machine code files.
  - Copy programs, to copy files from disk to tape, from tape to disk or from disk to disk.
  - Debug and trace programs to display and modify current memory contents, stop program execution at a breakpoint to display register contents and perform other program debugging functions.
  - Compare programs to examine two versions of the same file and display the differences.
- Interpreters to execute program in a procedure-oriented language such as BASIC.
- Compilers to convert source language programs (e.g., FORTRAN, Pascal, or COBOL) to executable machine code.

Operating System

The operating system (OS) is normally loaded into main memory when system power is turned on and remains there until the system is turned on and remains there until the system is shut down. It provides facilities for loading and executing programs that exist in external storage, for saving newly created programs or data files to external storage and for debugging programs. The extent of these facilities varies with the installation.

In systems that include floppy disk or cassette external storage, the OS includes file management routines to store and retrieve named files. In multiuser microcomputer systems, the OS allocate memory and I/O resources to each user, queues up user work requests and divides execution time equitably among the users.

A single-user microcomputer operating system does not require time and resource allocation; its main functions are file management.

The I/O Hardware/Software System

A microcomputer system is likely to have several I/O devices attached to it, the most common ones being:

- A console device, consisting of a CRT terminal, a typewriter terminal or a keyboard and memory-mapped video display.
- A line printer.
- One or more floppy or minifloppy disk drives for program and data storage.
- One or more cassette or cartridge tape drives.
- A modem or acoustic coupler for communication over the switched telephone network with remote terminals or with other computer systems.

Each bidirectional peripheral (not the line printer) may be regarded as two functionally separate components: an input device that sends data to the computer; and an output device that accepts data from the computer. Each input and output device in the system is connected to a separate I/O port and has different control and status signal requirements. How does an application program communicate with devices so as to ensure proper data delivery? We would not, for example, wish error messages or job statistics to be mixed in with document text on the line printer, nor should text or tables that are part of a program's main output appear on the console display.

It would be tedious and wasteful to write code in each program to handle the low-level details of input and output, such as interrogating a port to find its status or servicing interrupts. To reduce the programmer's involvement and to ensure uniform I/O handling, all input and output is performed by calls to the common entry point of the operating system. The OS interprets the parameters passed with the call and invokes the appropriate file management of I/O routine.

Flexibility in the I/O System is maintained by establishing *logical I/O devices*. A logical I/O device is a fixed address to which all I/O requests of a particular kind are directed—that is, console output is directed to the logical console output device; program listings or output data go to the logical list device; requests for operator input are directed to the logical console input device. A logical device is merely a switch point at which a link is established to a *physical device driver*. The physical device driver is a routine which handles all the details of input or output from the associated peripheral. The application program does not know or care which of several possible physical devices is supplying input or accepting output. Thus, the logical device routine acts like a multiposition switch, directing traffic flow. Typical logical devices (see Figure 2.1) are:

- *Console.* Accepts system commands or data input from the operator's keyboard and displays system responses on the typewriter or CRT screen.
- *Reader.* Accepts data or program file input from devices such as paper tape reader, or cassette.
- *Punch.* Sends data or program file output to devices such as paper tape punch or cassette.
- *Disk.* Handles input from and output to a hard or floppy disk.
- *List.* Sends output to a printer or other device.

Each physical device attached to the system has a corresponding physical device driver to perform control functions and transfer a character (or block of characters, in the case of the disk) provided by the calling program. These physical device drivers are linked to (or unlinked from) a logical device by *assign* commands. For example, consider a file to be read from disk and transferred over a telephone line to a remote computer. To assign the modem as the serial output device for list output, we might give the assign command:

LIST=MOD

where LIST represents the list logical device and MOD represents a physical device driver for a serial port that is connected to the modem. If a system command is given to list the file named ZINK, that file

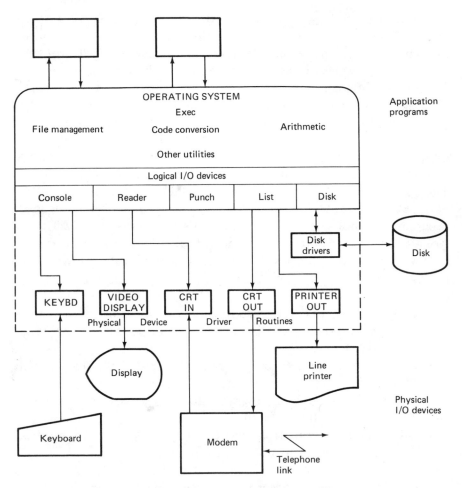

Figure 2.1. Operating system; block diagram.

would be brought into a buffer in main memory one block at a time and then transferred to the remote computer via the LIST logical device and the MOD physical device driver.

The routines using the LIST logical device accept a buffer address from the file management routines, establish character pointers, call the LIST logical device and report to the file management routines when all characters in the buffer have been sent. The MOD device driver, which is linked to the LIST logical device, accepts each character as it arrives from the disk buffer, interrogates the busy/free status of the modem, passes that character to the hardware for transmission and reports to the LIST routine when a new character can be accepted in the one-character hardware buffer. Figure 2.2 shows the complete sequence.

Microcomputer operating systems commonly have the four logical devices listed above, and allow four physical device drivers for each logical device. Some of these may be only stubs—that is, no logic, but a RET instruction to return control to the calling routine, followed by space for the user to implement his own drivers. Thus, up to 16 peripherals (in addition to floppy disk drives) may be permanently connected to the system. There is usually provision for linking the LIST logical device in tandem with the console logical device; also, there is nothing to prevent the user from modifying one of the physical device drivers to send output to two or more devices simultaneously.

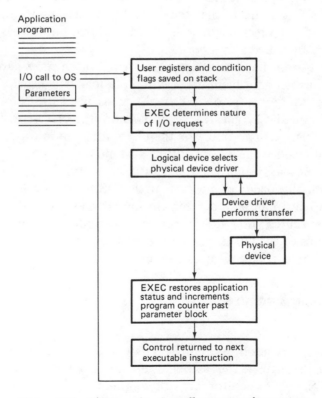

Figure 2.2. I/O transfers by calls to operating system.

2.2 BOOTSTRAPPING AND LOADING

The OS, a relatively complex program, occupies several thousand bytes. It must be loaded into main memory as soon as the system is turned on, to provide facilities for other programs. What is the mechanism to get it there?

In systems which have no read-only memory, the floppy disk controller contains a small bootstrap routine which loads one or more sectors from disk. When system power is first turned on, the bootstrap routine is executed automatically. The bootstrap reads in a more complex loader from the first sector of the disk. Then, according to the hardware design, control is automatically transferred to this loader, which reads in the rest of the OS. Each OS sector is checked and reread if an error is found. When all sectors of the OS have been read into memory, control is transferred to the OS starting address. The OS issues a prompt mark to the console. This is a special symbol, such as ">" to indicate that the system is ready and waiting for the operator to type in a command. These actions, initiated by turning on power, are called a *cold boot*.

If the system has a monitor or a BASIC interpreter permanently resident in read-only memory, a complete loader is usually included for other components to be brought in as needed. Upon turn-on, control immediately goes to the ROM monitor or to BASIC, which issues a prompt. The operator then types in a monitor (or BASIC) command to boot the disk operating system.

Sometimes a system or application program is run in memory space normally occupied by part of the OS, or the program requires the OS to be reinitialized after closing all files. A *warm boot* may then be executed; this differs from a cold boot, since only the *missing* portions of the OS are read from disk; control returns immediately to the OS, not to BASIC or to a monitor if either is present.

2.3 PROGRAMMING AIDS

Utilities

Text Editors.   A good text editor is essential for the creation of program source language files as well as documentation and other English language files. Text editors are of two kinds:

- Line-oriented.
- Context-oriented.

Both types enter data directly into memory, save the data as a named file and allow you to add, delete or modify text in an existing file. Usually tab expansion if provided—that is, the display routine substitutes spaces for each tab character found in the file.

Line-oriented editors number each text string terminated by a carriage return. An edit request specifies a line number, whereupon a further edit command causes that line to be modified accordingly.

A context-oriented editor does not number text lines, although it recognizes carriage return as a line terminator. All commands refer to an implied or visible character pointer which is positionable within the text, and operate on a specified number of characters or complete lines ahead of or behind this pointer. This type of editor is well suited to CRT terminals, where the cursor indicates the current position of the character pointer.

Text Formatters.   A text formatter reads a file created by a text editor and processes it for printing. Global commands are embedded in the text to specify how many characters per line and lines per page are to be printed. Special formatting commands embedded in the text determine whether the text is to be right-justified or printed as entered or single- or multiple-line spaced, and perform many other functions related to the appearance of the printed text. Some formatters provide automatic page numbering, heading and footing lines on each page, and commands that stop printing to allow the insertion of data from the console; "tagged" words or phrases are included in a table of contents or index.

Some word-processing programs combine both an editor and a formatter and allow one file to be printed while another is being created or edited. More often the editor and the formatter are separate programs. This allows more memory to be used for buffering the text, thereby speeding up search and replace operations during editing. Other advantages appear when the editor is used for creating program source files which are never processed by the formatter. However, when the system is primarily used for word-processing, the combined editor-formatter has advantages.

Print Programs. A hexadecimal dump program reads a binary program file, translates each byte into the two-character ASCII hexadecimal equivalent, and prints it. When a starting address is supplied, the print program inserts this at the start of the first line (the first line default is 0000). Sixteen bytes per line are printed; the address of each line is incremented by hex 10. An example is shown in Figure 2.3. A similar program is available to print the contents of disk sectors; here the addresses are relative to the start of the sector (Figure 2.4).

Another print program reads and prints an ASCII text file without making any modification. Useful options are: pause after every screenful; pause after every printed page; display of text with (or

```
DUMP SRT16.COM

0000 2A EF 01 22 02 02 2A 02 02 7C B7 1F 67 7D 1F 6F
0010 22 02 02 B4 CA 9B 01 EB 2A EF 01 CD E8 01 22 FE
0020 01 21 01 00 22 FC 01 2A FC 01 22 FA 01 2A 02 02
0030 EB 2A FA 01 19 22 00 02 2A FA 01 EB CD 9F 01 22
0040 04 02 2A 00 02 EB CD 9F 01 22 06 02 3A F7 01 47
0050 3A F6 01 2A 06 02 CD E3 01 EB 2A 04 02 3A F6 01
0060 CD E3 01 EB CD D7 01 B7 CA 87 01 FA 87 01 CD BB
0070 01 2A 02 02 EB 2A FA 01 CD E8 01 22 FA 01 CA 87
0080 01 DA 87 01 C3 2D 01 2A FC 01 23 22 FC 01 EB 2A
0090 FE 01 CD E8 01 DA 06 01 C3 27 01 2A F8 01 E9 3A
00A0 F1 01 CD AB 01 EB 2A F3 01 19 C9 21 00 00 06 08
00B0 29 07 D2 B6 01 19 05 C2 B0 01 C9 3A F5 01 47 3A
00C0 F1 01 90 47 2A 04 02 EB 2A 06 02 1A 4F 7E 12 71
00D0 13 23 05 C2 CB 01 C9 05 FA E2 01 1A 96 13 23 CA
00E0 D7 01 C9 85 6F D0 24 C9 7D 93 6F 7C 9A 67 C9 00
00F0 00 00 00 00 00 00 00 00 00 00 00 00 00 00 00 00
0100 00 00 00 00 00 00 00 00 00 00 00 00 00 00 00 00
```

(A.)

```
A>DDT
DDT VERS 1.4
-D100 1FF
0100 01 B6 0F C3 3D 01 43 4F 50 59 52 49 47 48 54 20  ....=.COPYRIGHT
0110 28 43 29 20 31 39 37 38 2C 20 44 49 47 49 54 41  (C) 1978, DIGITA
0120 4C 20 52 45 53 45 41 52 43 48 20 20 20 20 20 20  L RESEARCH
0130 44 44 54 20 56 45 52 53 20 31 2E 34 24 31 00 02  DDT VERS 1.4$1..
0140 C5 C5 11 30 01 0E 09 CD 05 00 C1 21 07 00 7E 3D  ...0.......!..~=
0150 90 57 1E 00 D5 21 00 02 78 B1 CA 65 01 0B 7E 12  .W...!..x..e..~.
0160 13 23 C3 58 01 D1 C1 E5 62 78 B1 CA 87 01 0B 7B  .#.X....bx.....{
0170 E6 07 C2 7A 01 E3 7E 23 E3 6F 7D 17 6F D2 83 01  ...z..~#.o}.o...
0180 1A 84 12 13 C3 69 01 D1 2E 00 E9 2A 7C 1D EB 0E  .....i.....*|...
0190 1A CD 67 1B C9 3E 0C D3 01 3E 08 D3 01 DB 01 07  ..g..>...>.....!
01A0 07 07 1F DA A9 08 C3 9D 08 DB 03 E6 7F C9 21 83  .........!..
01B0 1D 70 2B 71 2A 82 1D 44 4D CD A1 07 0E 3A CD 86  .p+q*..DM..:..
01C0 07 0E 20 CD 86 07 3A 5F 1D 32 84 1D 3A 60 1D 21  .. ...:_.2..:.!
01D0 84 1D BE DA F4 08 21 DE 1C 3A 84 1D BE D2 ED 08  .....!..:......
01E0 2A 84 1D 26 00 01 DF 1C 09 4E CD 86 07 21 84 1D  *..&.....N...!..
01F0 34 C2 CC 08 21 DE 1C 36 00 01 4A 01 00 9D AD 13  4...!...6..J.....
-
```

(B.)

Figure 2.3.   Hexadecimal dumps with memory addresses.

?

A>DISKDUMP

CP/M DUMP UTILITY VERS 1.3
COPYRIGHT 1978 BY S. J. SINGER

```
*  T 2 S 3-4
                DRIVE A - TRACK 2  SECTOR 3
0000  00 50 4D 4F 44 45 4D 20  20 48 45 58 00 00 00 4E  .PMODEM   HEX...N
0010  78 79 7A 7B 7C 7D 7E 7F  80 81 00 00 00 00 00 00  xyz{|}~. ........
0020  00 50 52 4F 4D 41 43 53  20 4C 49 42 00 00 00 07  .PROMACS  LIB....
0030  82 00 00 00 00 00 00 00  00 00 00 00 00 00 00 00  ........ ........
0040  00 50 52 4F 50 52 49 4E  54 43 4F 4D 00 00 00 54  .PROPRIN TCOM...T
0050  83 84 85 86 87 88 89 8A  8B 8C 8D 00 00 00 00 00  ........ ........
0060  00 52 45 53 4F 55 52 43  45 43 4F 4D 00 00 00 2D  .RESOURC ECOM...-
0070  8E 8F 90 91 92 93 00 00  00 00 00 00 00 00 00 00  ........ ........

                DRIVE A - TRACK 2  SECTOR 4
0080  E5 E5 E5 E5 E5 E5 E5 E5  E5 E5 E5 E5 E5 E5 E5 E5  eeeeeeee eeeeeeee
0090  E5 E5 E5 E5 E5 E5 E5 E5  E5 E5 E5 E5 E5 E5 E5 E5  eeeeeeee eeeeeeee
00A0  E5 E5 E5 E5 E5 E5 E5 E5  E5 E5 E5 E5 E5 E5 E5 E5  eeeeeeee eeeeeeee
00B0  E5 E5 E5 E5 E5 E5 E5 E5  E5 E5 E5 E5 E5 E5 E5 E5  eeeeeeee eeeeeeee
00C0  E5 E5 E5 E5 E5 E5 E5 E5  E5 E5 E5 E5 E5 E5 E5 E5  eeeeeeee eeeeeeee
00D0  E5 E5 E5 E5 E5 E5 E5 E5  E5 E5 E5 E5 E5 E5 E5 E5  eeeeeeee eeeeeeee
00E0  E5 E5 E5 E5 E5 E5 E5 E5  E5 E5 E5 E5 E5 E5 E5 E5  eeeeeeee eeeeeeee
00F0  E5 E5 E5 E5 E5 E5 E5 E5  E5 E5 E5 E5 E5 E5 E5 E5  eeeeeeee eeeeeeee
*
```

Figure 2.4. Hexadecimal dump of two diskette sectors.

without) line numbers—handy for relating compiler error messages
with text lines.

Debug/Trace Program.   A debug/trace program operates upon executable program code both statically and dynamically. The static facilities include the following commands:

- *Display.* Display on the console device the contents of memory, in hexadecimal (or sometimes octal), from a starting address to an ending address.
- *Substitute.* Examine successive memory locations one by one and display the contents. The operator may leave the contents unchanged or type in a new hexadecimal value for the current location.
- *Move.* Move the contents of a block of memory to a different area in memory.
- *Disassemble.* Examine a block of memory and display operation codes as assembly language mnemonics. Constants and absolute addresses are displayed in hexadecimal form.

Dynamic facilities allow a program under test to be executed under control of the debug/trace program. The program under test may be halted after every instruction, after a specified number of instructions, or when a specified address, called a *breakpoint*, is reached. A debug/trace program may also halt execution of the program under test when a register reaches a specified value, or if the program attempts to access a specified range of memory locations, etc. Whenever the program is halted, the debug/trace program displays the contents of all CPU registers. These facilities are helpful in first isolating a bug to a mudule or subroutine of the program under test, and then zooming in on that area to find the bug. A trace of 16 successive instructions is shown in Figure 2.5.

2.4 LANGUAGE PROCESSORS

Assemblers

An assembler converts a program source file consisting of assembly language commands into executable code. The programmer writes statements that are easier to understand than machine language in

```
-
-ISPEED.COM
-R
NEXT  PC
0180 0100
-T10
C0Z0M0E0I0 A=00 B=0000 D=0000 H=0000 S=0100 P=0100 MVI  C,09
C0Z0M0E0I0 A=00 B=0009 D=0000 H=0000 S=0100 P=0102 LXI  D,011D
C0Z0M0E0I0 A=00 B=0009 D=011D H=0000 S=0100 P=0105 CALL 0005
C0Z0M0E0I0 A=00 B=0009 D=011D H=0000 S=00FE P=0005 JMP  9D00
C0Z0M0E0I0 A=00 B=0009 D=011D H=0000 S=00FE P=9D00 JMP  A3A2
C0Z0M0E0I0 A=00 B=0009 D=011D H=0000 S=00FE P=A3A2 XTHL
C0Z0M0E0I0 A=00 B=0009 D=011D H=0108 S=00FE P=A3A3 SHLD AC44
C0Z0M0E0I0 A=00 B=0009 D=011D H=0108 S=00FE P=A3A6 XTHL
C0Z0M0E0I0 A=00 B=0009 D=011D H=0000 S=00FE P=A3A7 JMP  AD06
SPEED (0 FASTEST, 9 SLOWEST) ?
C0Z1M0E1I0 A=00 B=003F D=0000 H=0000 S=0100 P=0108 MVI  C,01
C0Z1M0E1I0 A=00 B=0001 D=0000 H=0000 S=0100 P=010A CALL 0005
C0Z1M0E1I0 A=00 B=0001 D=0000 H=0000 S=00FE P=0005 JMP  9D00
C0Z1M0E1I0 A=00 B=0001 D=0000 H=0000 S=00FE P=9D00 JMP  A3A2
C0Z1M0E1I0 A=00 B=0001 D=0000 H=0000 S=00FE P=A3A2 XTHL
C0Z1M0E1I0 A=00 B=0001 D=0000 H=010D S=00FE P=A3A3 SHLD AC44
C0Z1M0E1I0 A=00 B=0001 D=0000 H=010D S=00FE P=A3A6 XTHL *A3A7
```

Flags: Carry, zero, minus, even parity, interdigit carry

Figure 2.5. **Debugging trace of 16 consecutive instructions.**

hexadecimal notation; the assembler assigns absolute addresses to symbolic variables to eliminate the tedious chore of address assignment and bookkeeping.

An assembler generally performs two passes; each pass reads the entire source file once. The first pass allocates memory space for each instruction (1, 2, or 3 bytes, depending on the instruction type) and keeps track of the addresses. During this pass, the assembler constructs a symbol table containing named constants and their defined values, as well as labels and the addresses at which they occur. A label is any named point in the source program, such as the start of a subroutine or the destination of a branch instruction.

The second pass replaces symbolic operands and symbolic addresses by corresponding addresses and/or values found in the symbol table. Two new files are constructed: one contains the binary object code and, when complete, constitutes the machine language program that can be loaded into memory and run; the other is a listing, relating the original assembly language source statements to the ASCII hexadecimal equivalent of both the address where a command appears and the executable command for each source statement. A brief example of an assembly listing is shown in Figure 2.6.

The form of the object file varies. Assemblers for cassette operating systems often place the entire binary object file in memory and

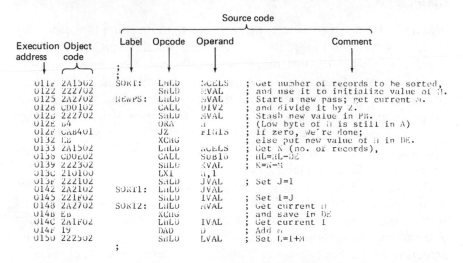

Figure 2.6.   Sample of assembly listing.

notify the operator to save it. Assemblers for disk operating systems generally write the file to disk in Intel Hex format—that is, in blocks of ASCII hexadecimal numbers representing the object code together with a count of the binary bytes represented by the block, the address at which the block is to be loaded and a check byte.

To create an executable file, a program-load/binary-translate utility is invoked to read the hex file, convert it to binary and load it at the correct place in memory. When loading is complete, it may also save the program on disk as an executable binary file. Thereafter, the load utility need not be used. The program is invoked and executed merely by giving its name as a command to the OS, which invokes a simpler loader (without binary translation) to read the binary program into memory and give it control. The Intel hex file may be retained just as a backup.

Macro assemblers allow the programmer to define a sequence of instructions and to give the sequence a name. Parameters on which the code sequence is to operate are given symbolic values. A sequence of this kind is called a *macroinstruction*, or simply a *macro*. Whenever the assembler encounters the macro name, it replaces the name with the full code sequence contained in the macro definition.

Other Languages

Assembly language is a little easier to use than machine language, but it still involves the programmer with much detail. Further, the mnemonics employed do not directly and obviously correspond to the logical operations performed. A simple comparison of two variables for equality may require four or more assembly language statements. Other programming languages have therefore been developed to ease the programmer's task. They are technically classed as *procedure-oriented languages* and sometimes called compiler languages or (erroneously) higher-level languages.

A program written in a procedure-oriented language is a sequence of English-like instructions. This *source* program is scanned once or more from beginning to end by a translator program; the translator generates a binary object machine language program in the native instruction set of the computer on which the program will run. Translator writers speak of this as the "target" computer. When the target computer is not the one on which the translator runs, the translator is called a *cross-assembler* if it handles assembly language, or a *cross-compiler* if it handles a compiler language.

Source Language Characteristics

The source program is English-like, using English words such as IF, THEN, PRINT, INPUT, GO TO, etc. However, the number of such words is limited; they can be used only in rigidly defined order and combinations. Punctuation symbols are not merely delimiters, but have a specific meaning. If the programmer writes statements that violate the rules of the language (the *syntax*), the translator normally flags these statements as errors and continues translation. In extreme cases, the error may be "fatal"; that is, the translator cannot continue. It then generates an error message to indicate the source line in which the error was detected and returns control to the OS.

POLs have many advantages:

- The programmer can concentrate on the logic of the application; the translator allocates space for variables, restates arithmetic or logic in machine language and handles input and output.
- Variables, functions and procedures are given pertinent names instead of the brief mnemonics or register designations of assembly language. Hence it is easier for us to understand the logic of the program.
- The data structures provided by the language represent the data in the form most suited to the application.
- The control structures for conditional branching, looping and parameter passing allow the creation of procedure sequences that can be modified without affecting other parts of the program. The program can thus be constructed from a number of relatively independent modules.

POLs have characteristics which are disadvantages in some applications:

- The source code is longer than comparable assembly language source code.
- Compilers are large (25K or more), so that source code for compilation often has to be brought into memory in sections.

- Compilers for micros do not do much optimization (removal of redundant instructions, etc.), so that compiled code is larger and slower than equivalent assembled code. This may become important in real-time applications.

In most cases, the application programmer chooses not between assembly language and a compiler language, but between compiler languages. Each has its own idiosyncrasies, but any one of them reduces the development time for a large program by a factor of 10 or more, when compared to assembly language.

Translators

Translators for converting source-language statements into executable machine code are of two types:

- Interpreters.
- Compilers.

The main difference between the interpreter and the compiler is the way in which each deals with the source statements:

- The interpreter works with one statement at a time and appears to execute it (if it does not reject it).
- The compiler translates the entire program into a machine language module. This module is later loaded and executed if the compiler has not flagged invalid statements.

To the programmer, the important difference is that the program furnished to the interpreter is executed immediately. Code generated by a compiler is in the form of one or more *relocatable object modules*. In a relocatable object module, addresses that are the targets of branch instructions are expressed as a displacement from the start of the module (which is usually set at 0000H). Each module is compiled separately. Then a *linking loader* is invoked to bring these relocatable object modules into memory in the desired order and assigns absolute addresses in real memory. This means that two modules, each 256 bytes long, both have addresses running from 00 to 0FFH in their relocatable form; however, after linking, the first module may have execution addresses running from 3100H to 31FFH while the second now has addresses running from 3200H to 32FFH. This linked assemblage of object modules may now be saved as a *load module*. It may be loaded by the operating system and executed. In this form, it will run only when properly loaded into the addresses assigned by the linking loader.

A compiler performs translation only once. The interpreter translates each source statement whenever it is encountered while running the program. Thus, in a loop that repeats 10 times, each statement in the loop is translated 10 times.

The interpreter has advantages and disadvantages. Both the interpreter and the source program are resident in memory throughout a run, but memory space is not a problem. Modern BASIC interpreters for microcomputers occupy 16K to 20K; in some cases the source program is stored in compressed format: all spaces are removed, and reserved words of the language (IF, PRINT, WHILE, etc.) are encoded as single bytes.

The chief advantage of an interpreter is that it may be *interactive*. The programmer enters a program and runs it in one shot. If errors occur, he corrects the source statements that are now in memory. A syntax error stops the interpreter, which produces an error message giving the line number where the error was detected. Some interpreters even go into an edit mode to prompt the programmer for the correction. The programmer retypes the line or corrects it and then gives the RUN command. If the program runs but gives erroneous results, TRACE and/or PRINT statements can be temporarily inserted at strategic points to see at which points correct results are produced and where they go bad. This reduces debugging time.

More steps are involved for a compiler: it flags all source statements that have bad syntax, printing the error messages at the end of translation. The programmer corrects the bad statements, using an editor, and then recompiles. Further errors may be uncovered by the linking loader before the first run. When a seemingly correct machine language program is produced, errors in the logic may still produce erroneous results. For each logic error caught thereafter, three runs are required: compile, link and run—which is time-consuming.

Compilers are generally larger than interpreters—32K or more, whereas a linking loader may occupy 10K or more. Perhaps the ideal solution, available in one dialect of BASIC, is to use an interpreter for development and debugging, and a compiler to create fast, compact machine language code from the debugged source. The compiled version of the program runs 20 to 30 times faster than the interpreted source.

Microcomputer Procedure-Oriented Languages

BASIC. Basic was the first language implemented on a microcomputer. Most microcomputer people (perhaps 80 percent) write their programs in BASIC, because it is easy to learn and use.

Microprocessor chips were initially regarded by the industry as process controllers. In 1974, however, MITS, Inc. marketed a general purpose microcomputer kit (the Altair 8800) based on the Intel 8080 chip, and commissioned a team of consultants to write a 4K BASIC interpreter for it. The principal members of that team later founded Microsoft, Inc., which now markets BASIC interpreters and compilers for most microcomputers on the market.

The original version of BASIC, produced at Dartmouth College as a tool for teaching the art of programming, was easy to learn (the name is an acronym of Beginner's All-purpose Symbolic Instruction Code) though rather primitive. The original Dartmouth statements are present in all modern dialects, but the accretions for string and array handling, file handling and editing all work differently in each version. Programs written in one dialect are not transportable to other versions without modification. However, the modern dialects are powerful and well-suited to many applications. It has for some years been the standard programming language for microcomputers, though today a far wider choice is available.

Pascal. This language was designed by Niklaus Wirth of the Federal Institute of Technology (ETH) at Zurich, Switzerland, as a tool for teaching not just the elements of coding but also sound program design and construction practices. It has a following because programs (either your own or somebody else's) are easy to read and maintain. If you can read it, it's easy to change. In particular, the emphasis of the language is on flexibility in data structures and on tight control structures. In BASIC, all variables are global—that is, any variable may be accessed and modified by any part of the program. Subroutines are merely instruction sequences that can be called from any part of the program, and there is no restriction on the destination of a branch.

Pascal emphasizes data declarations, functions and procedures. Every variable must be declared by name and type (character, integer, real, etc.) before it can be used. A procedure is an instruction sequence having only one entry and one exit; variables declared within the procedure definition are local to that procedure. Functions are procedures which return a logical or arithmetic value. Microcomputer implementations generally do not allow forward references; as a consequence, some users find it annoying that the main program loop containing most of the major decisions comes at the very end of the listing. This, however, is of minor consequence compared to the ease with which individual procedures and functions can be modified without affecting the remainder.

Pascal was designed to be completely transportable. For this reason, the "target" of the compiler is a hypothetical pseudo-machine (a P-machine) with a simple and standard instruction set. The P-code produced by the compiler for this machine is then translated by an interpreter implemented for the hardware machine on which the program is to run. If the Pascal standards are strictly followed, the P-code version of the program can indeed be run without modification on any machine from an IBM 3033 to an 8-bit microcomputer.

Most implementations of Pascal for microcomputers are subsets of the full language, and variations are already starting to appear. Some versions, for example, compile native 8080 or Z80 machine code instead of P-code. This results in relatively small compilers and fast, compact object code. The program may no longer be transportable without modification, however, because of the manner in which these compilers handle console and file I/O. The UCSD version generates P-code and has been implemented for a number of microprocessors, including the Western Digital Pascal Micro-Engine, which is a hardware implementation of the P-machine and executes P-code as if it were machine language. UCSD Pascal is probably the most widely used version.

C. C provides flexibility of data structure and excellent control structures. All program segments (including the main program) are treated as functions—that is, they have one entry and one exit, and return a logical or arithmetic value, though this is not always used. Statements can become very dense because calls to functions may form part of an expression. A typical statement is:

putchar(c=inp(MODDATA) & 0x7f);

Here "putchar" is a function to display a character on the console; its argument is c, which is assigned to the character returned by function inp, an input routine operating on an I/O port MODDATA. The character returned by inp is logically ANDed with hex 7F to strip off the parity bit before being put into c.

The C language is well-suited to system software, because it allows intimate contact with the hardware, as well as a high level of abstraction for good program design. However, it does not forbid the use of mnemonic rather than descriptive names for variables, and poor choice of names combined with dense expressions can make a program very difficult to understand.

Two C compilers have been implemented for 8080/Z80 machines using the CP/M operating system. Both produce compact, fast object code from substantial subsets of the full C language. A compiler for a smaller subset and designed for cassette-based systems has been published. This is written in C, and can be bootstrapped into any microcomputer for which the "tiny c" interpreter has been implemented (8080/Z80, 6800, 6502, LSI-11).

FORTRAN. This warhorse, and the RATFOR preprocessor which allows "structured" statements to be converted into standard FORTRAN statements, are available for 8080/Z80 and 6800 machines. The compilers provide a standard ANSI subset of the language, but require at least 56K of memory.

COBOL is also available for 8080/Z80 machines with 64K of memory. Three compilers which run under CP/M provide all of the level 1 ANSI 1974 subset, and most of the level 2 features. There is also a COBOL compiler for all Radio Shack models running under TRS-DOS.

ALGOL-60. One compiler is available for 8080/Z80 machines. It includes almost all the ALGOL '60 Report, as well as many extensions such as string handling and disk I/O to make it capable of running in 24K of memory.

PL/1.   One compiler is available for 8080/Z80 machines. It provides a substantial subset of the full language and is supplied with a library of 300 callable subroutines, a linker, a library manager and a cross-reference generator.

Other languages for microcomputers include APL (a powerful array processor designed for engineers), FORTH and STOIC, TRAC (designed primarily for word-processing), PILOT (designed for computer-aided instruction), and LISP (a list-processing language).

II
ENTRY AND PRESENTATION

3
Keyboards

3.1 COMMUNICATING WITH THE COMPUTER

The Keyboard as Input Device

Interaction between the computer and the human has long been by keyboard for input and by a computer-driven trypewriter or a CRT screen for output. Written language uses a small number of symbols which are easily encoded in digital form and yet can be combined in innumerable ways to convey meaning. From the human point of view, written language is neither the best nor the quickest way of communicating. Speech is fast and does not require manual dexterity or typing skill.

Although speech-recognition devices are currently available, they are still expensive. With them a microcomputer can be trained to recognize spoken words—but may not recognize them when spoken by a person other than the original "trainer". There are also devices which convert digital patterns in the computer memory into recognizable speech. Both, however, have limited vocabulary and use a considerable amount of the computer's resources. The truly conversational computer may be on its way but is still quite a long way off. The keyboard or variations of it is likely to remain the primary input device for quite a few years.

Keyswitch Mechanism

The aim of this mechanism is to generate and transmit to the computer a code each time a key is pressed. A unique code is associated with the key; this is the machine language representation of the letter or numeral or symbol whose label is engraved on the keytop. The mechanism should be reliable and send the one and only proper code when the key is pressed. Figure 3.1 shows the general operation of a keyboard.

The input keyboard is composed of a set of labeled push-button switches; each closes a pair of electrical contacts. The nature of this contact is of considerable importance and should:

- Be reliable.
- Have long life (millions of operations).
- Feel right.

We will consider the last effect later, under the heading of human engineering; we now examine the different types of switch mechanisms in modern keyboards.

Mechanical. On early key switches a plunger is attached to the keytop; when the key is pressed, the plunger forces a platinum contact on a flexible metal spring against a similar platinum contact on a fixed arm, as shown in Figure 3.2. This is like a relay contact. The arrangement is bulky; the unprotected contacts are subject to corrosion and oxidation, and dust can be trapped there so that they become unreliable.

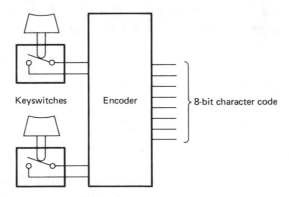

Figure 3.1. General operation of a keyboard.

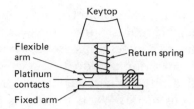

Figure 3.2. Mechanical key switch.

The modern equivalents are the cross-point switch (Figure 3.3) and the reed switch (Figure 3.4). The cross-point switch consists of two springy wires. One is fixed to the mounting plate and is bowed slightly upward. The other is mounted at a right angle so that it crosses above the other with a gap between them. When the key is pressed, the plunger forces the movable spring into contact with the fixed spring. The area of contact is small, and pressure is concentrated there. The slight bowing of the fixed spring creates a wiping action between the two springs, which are thus to some extent self-cleaning. Both springs are gold-plated to resist corrosion. This type of switch

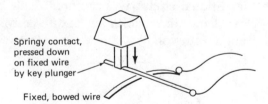

Figure 3.3. Cross-point key switch.

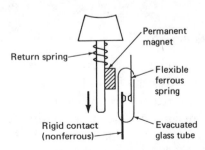

Figure 3.4. Reed key switch.

provides better contact than does the relay type, but it is usually open and hence is still vulnerable to dust. It is, however, inexpensive.

For the reed switch, the contact arms are sealed within a glass tube to protect them from corrosion and dust. The glass tube may either be evacuated or be filled with an inert gas such as argon. At least one of the arms is of ferrous metal. When the key is pressed, a magnet moves down outside the glass tube, and the magnetic field penetrating the glass pulls the flexible ferrous arm into firm contact with the stiff nonferrous arm.

Capacitive. Many modern keyboards use keyswitches in which no contact "closure" is used; instead, the switch element consists of a variable capacitor. In Figure 3.5, the fixed plate is etched on the printed circuit board; the movable plate is of flexible metal and is deformed by the key pressure so that it moves toward the fixed plate, thereby increasing the capacitance between the two. It does not make contact because the two are insulated by a thin sheet of dielectric material such as mica. This mechanism can be hermetically sealed to prevent the entry of dust and corrosive particles. The mechanism itself is simple, but additional circuitry is required to detect the relatively small and slow change in capacitance, and to convert it into an abrupt rise (or fall) in output voltage.

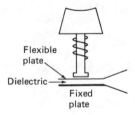

Flexible
plate

Dielectric

Fixed
plate

Figure 3.5. Capacitive key switch.

Hall-Effect. Another contactless electronic switch widely used in the more expensive keyboard is the Hall-effect switch. This consists of a hermetically sealed transistor whose conductance is dependent upon the strength of the magnetic field surrounding it. Pressing the key (Figure 3.6) pushes a permanent magnet attached to the plunger into the proximity of the Hall-effect transistor. When the magnetic field induced by the magnet reaches the threshold value, the transistor's

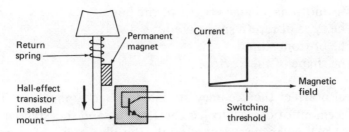

Figure 3.6.   Hall effect key switch.

conductance switches abruptly from almost zero to maximum value, producing an abrupt wavefront. This mechanism is more expensive than the capacitive type, but the supporting circuitry is less complex. The total cost per key is therefore approximately the same for both types.

Key Bounce

When a single keystroke causes several repetitions of the character to appear on the display, the effect is called *bounce*. The worst examples occur in mechanical switches open to the atmosphere. The rubbing action of the moving contact tends to clean the contacts, but in a dusty or polluted atmosphere specks of dirt or areas of corrosion can cause contact resistance to vary over such a wide range during the keystroke that the interface logic interprets the variations as multiple keystrokes. In a magnetically operated reed switch, vibration of the moving arm can cause actual separation of the contacts one or more times after the initial closure.

The Radio Shack TRS-80 and the Apple II microcomputers are vulnerable to key bounce, since they both have unsealed mechanical keyswitches. Key bounce can be eliminated by hardware, or software, or a combination of both, acting to delay transfer of the character code to the CPU until the key contacts have had time to stabilize. The delay time is usually a few milliseconds.

Human Engineering Considerations

A number of factors have an effect on the ease with which the keyboard can be used:

- The motional characteristics of the key.
- The type of return spring used.
- The bottom stop.
- The shape of the keytop.

These also affect the accuracy attainable when typing fast. The relative placement of characters has some effect, and so a standard layout for each major language is used; only the placement of punctuation and symbols differs from one (English language) keyboard to the next.

Persons who are used to a typewriter generally prefer a key mechanism that provides little resistance at first and then gives a definite change of feel that signals completion of the keystroke. This may be either a sudden stop after a relatively light pressure or a "click" before the key is all the way down. Keys that come to a slow halt when the return spring is compressed until all its coils are touching generally have a "soggy" feel that makes fast and accurate typing difficult. $\propto$

A point which deserves further consideration by keyboard manufacturers, because it has a considerable effect on ease of operation, is the placement of special function keys such as those for margin setting, restriction of alphabetic characters to uppercase, and pitch selection of 10 or 12 characters per inch. On a CRT terminal, there are also keys to control cursor or for calling up special screen displays. A terminal (or keyboard) is often used for several purposes. There is a frequent need to enter mixed uppercase letters and numerals; for this reason the uppercase restrict key should be close to the main section of the keyboard (not tucked away under a cover). It is desirable to have all such functions available on keys similar to the alphanumeric keys and close to them. The keyboard shown in Figure 3.7 has considered these needs.

3.2 ENCODERS

A physical keystroke is converted to an abrupt change in voltage by the keyswitch. This change can be sensed by a computer system, using a separate conductor for each key, with a common return. This is occasionally done where only a few keys are provided (a numeric keypad, for example), but it would be a clumsy and uneconomic method for a full alphanumeric keyboard with 60 to 80 keys. Instead,

Figure 3.7. Well-arranged keyboard with function keys.

the contact closure of each key is encoded as a number that can conveniently be handled by the computer.

Most microcomputers have registers to operate upon numbers that are 8 or 16 bits long. Eight bits can be combined in 256 different patterns; this value is large enough to accommodate patterns representing all the printable characters of European languages as well as patterns representing editing or equipment control functions. For this reason, electronic keyboards contain encoding circuitry that generates a unique 8-bit pattern for each key.

Output Codes in General Use

First, a few definitions. To each character in the alphabet (which includes letters, numerals, punctuation, and control or nonprintable characters) assign a unique combination of 1s and 0s. These are commonly known as character codes (or simply codes). Consider now the entire set of codes for the alphabet. There are many code sets; they may be classified, according to the number of bits in each character, as 5-bit, 6-bit, 7-bit or 8-bit code sets.

Two widely used code/sets are the American Standard Code for Information Interchange (ASCII) and Extended Binary Coded Decimal Information Code (EBCDIC). The ASCII code is used by all communications networks using leased telephone lines and data concentrators or message-switching computers; EBCDIC is used by IBM computers and their relatives which are plug-compatible mainframes. Minicomputers and microcomputers use ASCII both internally and for communication with the console and remote terminals. ASCII is a 7-bit code which represents 128 letters, numerals and symbols as shown in Table 3-1; an eighth bit is generally used for parity to detect transmission errors. EBCDIC is an 8-bit code that represents up to 256 letters, numerals and symbols, as in Table 3-2, though it is seldom that all 256 are in use in any one system. Keyboard/printer terminals based on the IBM Selectric I/O typewriter use a 6-bit subset of EBCDIC shown in Table 3-3. The 6 bits provide only 64 patterns, but two of these represent up shift and down shift, to tell the receiver

Table 3-1

b_4	b_3	b_2	b_1	COLUMN / ROW	0	1	2	3	4	5	6	7
				$b_7 b_6 b_5$ →	$^0 0_0$	$^0 0_1$	$^0 1_0$	$^0 1_1$	$^1 0_0$	$^1 0_1$	$^1 1_0$	$^1 1_1$
					0	1	2	3	4	5	6	7
0	0	0	0	0	NUL	DLE	SP	0	@	P	`	p
0	0	0	1	1	SOH	DC1	!	1	A	Q	a	q
0	0	1	0	2	STX	DC2	"	2	B	R	b	r
0	0	1	1	3	ETX	DC3	#	3	C	S	c	s
0	1	0	0	4	EOT	DC4	$	4	D	T	d	t
0	1	0	1	5	ENQ	NAK	%	5	E	U	e	u
0	1	1	0	6	ACK	SYN	&	6	F	V	f	v
0	1	1	1	7	BEL	ETB	'	7	G	W	g	w
1	0	0	0	8	BS	CAN	(	8	H	X	h	x
1	0	0	1	9	HT	EM	)	9	I	Y	i	y
1	0	1	0	10	LF	SUB	*	:	J	Z	j	z
1	0	1	1	11	VT	ESC	+	;	K	[	k	{
1	1	0	0	12	FF	FS	,	<	L	\	l	¦
1	1	0	1	13	CR	GS	–	=	M	]	m	}
1	1	1	0	14	SO	RS	.	>	N	^	n	~
1	1	1	1	15	SI	US	/	?	O	——	o	DEL

Table 3-2

Most Significant Digits

Hexadecimal \ (MSD→)	Binary	0	1	2	3	4	5	6	7	8	9	A	B	C	D	E	F
	Binary	0000	0001	0010	0011	0100	0101	0110	0111	1000	1001	1010	1011	1100	1101	1110	1111
0	0000	NUL	DLE	LF only	ESC F	SP	&	—	<				FF	SP		–	0
1	0001	SOH	X-ON	FS	CAN	7ESC J	ESC D	/	:	a	j		\ [1]	A	J	S	1
2	0010	STX	DC2	GS	ESC X	⊥	□	⌐	|	b	k	s	{ [1]	B	K	T	2
3	0011	ETX	X-OFF	RS	ESC P	ESC LF		⌐	—	c	l	t	} [1]	C	L	U	3
4	0100	EOT	DC4	US	ESC U	⌐	⊤	→	∀	d	m	u	[[1]	D	M	V	4
5	0101	HT	LF NL	EM	ESC Z	ε	○	ω	∧	e	n	v	] [1]	E	N	W	5
6	0110	ACK	SYN [8]	/	ESC)			∩	∪	f	o	w	NUL	F	O	X	6
7	0111	BEL	ETB	<	ESC T	Δ			>	g	p	x		G	P	Y	7
8	1000	EOM BS	CAN	=	ESC S	~		⟨ [1]	:	h	q	y		H	Q	Z	8
9	1001	ENQ	EM	CR only	ESC E	¢ [2]	!	⟨ [1]	>	i	r	z		I	R		9
A	1010	NAK	SUB	EOT	ESC C	.	$	⟨ [1]	:			— [6]		[7]			×
B	1011	VT	ESC	BS	ESC O	∨	*	,	#				| [6]				÷
C	1100	FF	FS	)	X-ON	(	)	%	@				| [6]				↑
D	1101	CR	GS	HT	X-OFF	+	;	|	'				Lost 6 Data				↓
E	1110	SO	RS	LF only	ESC R	| [2]	⌐ [2]	∧	=				⌐ [6]				
F	1111	SI	US	SUB	ESC CR	⌐ [2]	⌐ [2]	?	"								DEL

Least Significant Digits

Table 3-3

				1	2	1	2	1	2	1	2	←BIT POSITION
BIT POSITION→ 3	4	5	6	B	A	B	A	B	A	B	A	←BIT VALUE
BIT VALUE → 8	4	2	1	0	0	0	1	1	0	1	1	
0	0	0	0	SP		@		—		&		
0	0	0	1	1		/		j		a		
0	0	1	0	2		s		k		b		
0	0	1	1	3		t		l		c		
0	1	0	0	4		u		m		d		
0	1	0	1	5		v		n		e		
0	1	1	0	6		w		o		f		
0	1	1	1	7		x		p		g		
1	0	0	0	8		y		q		h		
1	0	0	1	9		z		r		i		
1	0	1	0	0								
1	0	1	1	EOA =				$				
1	1	0	0	RCD		PRNT		RST		READ		
1	1	0	1			INDEX		CR/LF		TAB		
1	1	1	0	UC SHIFT				BKSP		LC SHIFT		
1	1	1	1	EOT		PREFIX		IDLE		CD		

LOWER CASE

SP	¢	—	+
=	?	J	A
<	S	K	B
;	T	L	C
:	U	M	D
%	V	N	E
'	W	O	F
>	X	P	G
*	Y	Q	H
(	Z	R	I
)			
"	l	!	¬

UPPER CASE

that characters which follow are upper- or lowercase, respectively. The code set also includes codes for machine control functions.

To summarize, when a key is pressed on the keyboard, there is available at the output connector in parallel format:

- A unique code corresponding to that key.
- A level or pulse to signal that some key has been pressed.

Encoding Mechanisms

Now consider how an encoder converts a single contact closure (from pressing a key) to an 8-bit pattern and a separate pulse.

Static Encoder. A simple keyboard encoding scheme for 7-bit ASCII (without parity generation) is shown in Figure 3.8. Two sets of conductors are arranged in a matrix; the horizontal wires provide the 7-bit output pattern and, with no keys pressed, are all held at +5V by pullup resistors R1 through R7. One vertical wire, grounded when the key is pressed, is provided for each keyswitch. Encoding diodes

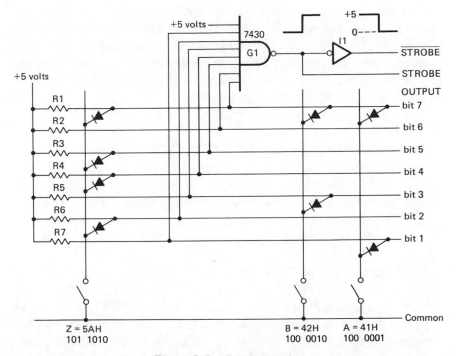

Figure 3.8. Static encoder.

connect a vertical (input) matrix wire with each horizontal wire that should change state to provide the proper output pattern.

The ASCII code for A, for example, is 41H (binary 100 0001). When the A key is pressed, its vertical wire is grounded and pulls horizontal lines 7 and 1 down to ground through the two diodes. The resulting bit pattern on the output lines is 011 1110, directly usable for negative logic (where a 0 represents an active line, and a 1 an idle line). The pattern can be complemented by inverters to obtain the positive logic pattern 100 0001. A different encoder design could produce the positive pattern directly. In practice, most keyboards generate a negative pattern because this makes it easier to detect malfunctions (an open circuit is perceived by TTL chips as a high input).

Each switch line has diodes to pull down the appropriate output lines to ground. The Z key, for example, pulls down bits 7, 5, 4 and 2, generating the negative logic bit pattern 010 0101, which can be inverted to its complement 101 1010 (5AH, ASCII Z).

The key-pressed strobe is produced by 8-input NAND gate G1: input is from the seven output lines of the matrix and +5V. If no key is pressed, all the input lines are high, and the output of gate G1 is therefore low. However, if some key is pressed, at least one input of gate G1 is pulled low, thereby driving the STROBE output high. For negative logic, STROBE is inverted by I. .

This matrix scheme is not practical as shown:

1. It does not allow generation of the all-zeros code.
2. If two keys are pressed at the same time, the output is not correct for either of them. It is the logical OR of the two patterns. Lifting one key allows the correct pattern for the other to appear on the data lines; however, it is not detected by the computer because no strobe is generated.

Practical versions of this static encoder use combinatorial logic instead of diodes to create output, and have additional logic to provide *rollover*—the ability to distinguish which key is pressed first when two keys are pressed in rapid succession. Even if they remain down after the first pressure, rollover ensures that the correct code and a separate strobe are generated for both keys, in the order in which they were pressed.

Lockout and Rollover.   An encoder has *N*-key lockout if pressing one key prevents *N* other key closures from being detected until the first key is released. An encoder has rollover if it correctly encodes one or more keys pressed before the first key is released. Two-key rollover is common; it is easy and inexpensive to provide. However, keyboards with two-key rollover may encode erroneously if three or more key closures overlap.

N-key rollover ensures that multiple key closures are detected and encoded in the order in which keys were pressed. It is expensive to store the pattern for each key the instant it is pressed and then release the stored pattern and generate a new strobe as soon as, but not until, the previous key is released. Special precautions are needed to prevent the generation of spurious patterns via "phantom" paths through the multiple key closures.

Scanning Encoder. We now discuss an encoding scheme which provides N-key rollover, allows flexibility in keyboard layout and permits any desired code set to be generated without any changes to the circuit board on which the keys are mounted. This is the scanning encoder.

Figure 3.9 shows a block diagram of a scanning encoder. The switch matrix has 16 vertical wires (VO to VF) crossing 8 horizontal wires (H0 to H7). Visualize a keyswitch over each intersection, so that pressing the key connects together the horizontal and vertical wires at this intersection, as shown in the inset. This scheme shows one way in which we might generate the standard 128-character subset of the ASCII code, with a key for each character. In this scheme, a key is positioned in the matrix according to the nibbles (half-bytes) which

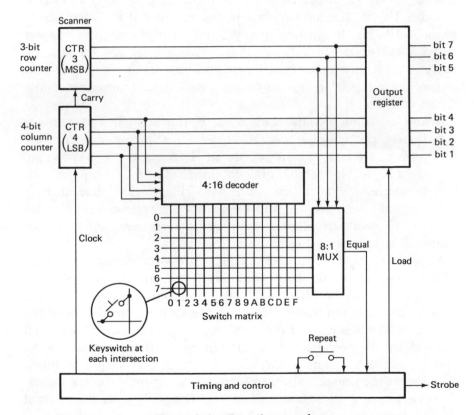

Figure 3.9. Scanning encoder.

compose its pattern. The horizontals are for the more significant nibble, and the verticals, for the less significant. Thus, the key for C, whose code is 43H, is a switch bridging H4 and V3. In practice, the arrangement of the matrix takes account of the number of keys provided and modifications introduced by the SHIFT and CONTROL keys (omitted here) which allow more than one pattern to be generated by one key.

The scanner shown in Figure 3.9 consists of a 7-bit counter which receives clock pulses at a rate of approximately 50 kilohertz as long as no key is pressed. The four least significant bits are decoded by a 4-to-16-line decoder which places a signal on exactly one of the 16 matrix column wires. The three most significant bits address an 8-to-1-line multiplexer which selects exactly one of the horizontal matrix row wires. Thus, as the count increases from 0 through 15 (hex 0 through F), all the keyswitches in matrix row 0 are successively probed. If some keyswitch in row 0 has been pressed, the decoder signal is transferred from the corresponding vertical wire through the switch to the row 0 horizontal wire and appears at the multiplexer output terminal. If no key has been pressed, the column counter continues to advance.

When the column count reaches hex F, the next clock pulse resets it to 0 and a carry pulse is generated to advance the row counter. Now the keyswitches in row 1 are probed in the same way. The rows are scanned and, within each row, the columns are scanned until the combined column/row count becomes hex 7F. At that time all keyswitches have been probed (and found open). The next clock pulse resets both counters to 00, and the process starts over, repeating continuously as long as no key is pressed.

Suppose that we press the C key. The row wire (4) and the column wire (3) that define the key coordinates in the matrix are connected together; this has no effect until the row counter and the column counter are simultaneously addressing the matrix coordinates of the depressed key (4H and V3 for the C key). At that instant, the signal emitted by the decoder passes through the switch contacts to the multiplexer and appears at the EQUAL multiplexer output terminal. This causes the timing and control logic to interrupt the clock pulses, thereby stopping the counter. The LOAD signal opens the internal parallel input gates of the output register and loads this register with the bit pattern produced by the stopped row/column counters. After a few microseconds delay, to ensure that all register bits have settled to their final value, a key-pressed strobe is generated. The counter remains halted for as long as the key is held down.

If a second key is pressed before the first is released, no action takes place. Only when the first key is released is the EQUAL signal from the multiplexer cut off. The scanner starts counting again from where it left off until it addresses the row and column of the second key pressed. The scanner then stops once more, and a new key-pressed strobe is generated.

Note, however, that if three or more keys are pressed in such rapid succession that their switch closures overlap, they are not necessarily encoded in the correct order. The first one detected is correctly encoded; when that key is released, the scanner advances until the next key closure in the matrix sequence is found. This may be the third or fourth key pressed, rather than the second. To avoid errors due to three or more simultaneous key closures, full N-key rollover circuitry is required.

The keys could be wired into the matrix in such a manner that their matrix coordinates were also the desired code. However, from the manufacturer's point of view this would have the same drawbacks as the static encoder; that is, the printed circuit board on which the keys and matrix wiring are mounted would be valid only for one specific key layout, and the wiring might be so tortuous as to make the printed circuit artwork very expensive.

The count at which the scanner stops when a key is pressed is loaded into the output register, but it does not necessarily bear any relation to the desired ASCII code. To design the scanner more efficiently, view the matrix coordinates or scanner count as arbitrary values. The scanner count is converted into the character code by a table in read-only memory (ROM).

The SHIFT and CONTROL keys are not connected to the matrix; they produce signal signals. The scanner register output lines are applied to the lower eight address lines of the ROM, and the code found at the addressed location is gated onto the data lines for loading into the character register. The SHIFT and CONTROL signals are placed on high-order address lines of the ROM. Hence the scanner register addresses ROM locations:

- 0 through 127 (hex 00 through 7F, neither SHIFT nor CONTROL pressed).
- 128 through 255 (hex 80 through FF, with SHIFT pressed).
- Or 256 through 383 (hex 100 through 17F, with CONTROL pressed).

One printed circuit board serves a family of keyboards; each keyboard may have a different layout and character set; the only change necessary is to plug in the proper ROM and to supply appropriately engraved keytops.

The scanning encoder is in almost universal use in high-quality keyboards. With large-scale integration (LSI), the scanner, decoder, multiplexer, strobe generator, conversion ROM and output buffers can be manufactured in a single low-price 40-pin package. The 2376 chip produces the full ASCII code set from an 8 X 11 matrix, with two-key rollover: the 3600 has N-key rollover (where N is not specified, it implies as many keys as are on the keyboard). The 7837 and the 7301 both produce 8-bit EBCDIC code from a keyboard. The Mostek 2503 performs ASCII-EBCDIC and EBCDIC-ASCII conversion.

3.3 SPECIAL-PURPOSE KEYS

In addition to the keys corresponding to the character set native to the terminal or microcomputer, most keyboards include additional keys that perform control functions associated with internal editing features or operating system functions of the host computer. The control functions normally provided fall into three groups:

- Code modification.
- Communications control.
- Local control.

Code Modification

SHIFT and CONTROL, in combination with an alphanumeric key, each produce an additional code. In the ASCII code chart, Table 3.1, the characters appear in a matrix of 8 columns and 16 rows. Each column corresponds to one of the eight possible values of the three most significant bits (b7, b6, b5) of the ASCII code set. Within any particular column, the characters are arranged in ascending numeric or alphabetic order, which is also ascending order of the 16 possible values (0 through F) of the four least significant bits (b4, b3, b2, b1) of the ASCII code set. There are four major groups of two columns each.

The first group, columns 0 and 1, contains machine control codes which represent carriage return, line feed, vertical tab (about 6 lines), form feed (1 page), horizontal tab, backspace and bell. The remaining codes are for transmission protocols or communications. ESC (escape) often indicates to a program that the character immediately following is not to be printed but used as a parameter to initiate some special function (such as invoking plotting activities).

The second group, columns 2 and 3, consists of the space, numerals and standard symbols. The third group (columns 4 and 5) contains the uppercase letters and some optional symbols. The fourth group (columns 6 and 7) contains the lowercase letters and the remaining optional symbols.

All ASCII control codes have the bit pattern 00X XXXX (where X may be 0 or 1). The CONTROL key forces bits b7 and b6 to 0, regardless of what additional key is pressed. Some keyboards have extra keys for the commonly used protocol codes, but where these are not provided, the CONTROL key allows them to be generated. Thus, the SOH code (000 0001) is generated by holding down CONTROL and then striking ! or A; the DC1 code is generated by holding down CONTROL and striking 1, or Q.

SHIFT causes the key pressed along with it to generate one of two printable characters. The choice is one of these:

- Lowercase (a, unshifted) or uppercase (A, shifted).
- A numeral (4, unshifted) or a symbol ($, shifted).
- One of two symbols (- unshifted or = shifted).

The upper- and lowercase codes for a letter differ only in the setting of bit b6 (0 for upper, 1 for lower). However, SHIFT for a numeric or symbol key affects bit b5, so that 3 becomes #. The SPACE bar and the numeral 0 always generate 20H and 30H, respectively, regardless of SHIFT setting. On keyboards for a 64-character subset of the ASCII set, SHIFT usually forces bit b6 to 0 for letters, and bit b5 to 0 for symbols. On keyboards that generate a 128-character subset, the character is partially decoded and a binary subtractor subtracts either 10H from codes below 41H, or 20H from all higher codes when SHIFT is pressed. Bit forcing does not work, because symbols (e.g., ` { ~ ¦) are in the group containing lowercase letters.

For a scanning encoder with ROM code conversion, SHIFT or CONTROL merely causes a different block of ROM locations to be accessed for the individual character key; the contents of those locations may vary from keyboard to keyboard. The customary static encoder associates * with :, and + with;, whereas with a scanning encoder one usually finds the * over the 8 and the: over the ;, as on a regular typewriter.

Where the keyboard is used for programming and for word processing, it is desirable to have a modified form of shift, variously known as UPPER CASE LOCK, ALPHA, TELETYPE LOCK or CAPS LOCK. This key locks and unlocks on alternate pressures. In the locked position, alpha keys generate only uppercase codes. However, numeric and symbol keys are not affected; they are controlled in the usual way by the standard SHIFT key. The UPPER CASE LOCK allows the entry of mixed uppercase letters and numerals without shifting. The standard SHIFT LOCK is used during word-processing entry to capitalize a string of characters. Few keyboards have both a SHIFT LOCK and an UPPER CASE LOCK; keyboard sales brochures are often regrettably ambiguous about the action of the LOCK key provided.

Communications Control

ASCII control codes in columns 0 and 1 of the chart do not print (though they sometimes appear on a CRT screen); they are needed for communication between the computer and a remote terminal or another computer. For example, ACK indicates proper reception. The significance of the control codes depends upon the protocol (see Chapter 14). Some keyboards provide extra keys which generate only these transmission control codes. Where dedicated keys are absent, the codes may be generated from alpha or numeric keys by holding down CONTROL while striking the key.

ASCII keyboards usually have a BREAK key; this does not generate a code but forces the communications line to the idle state for a period of 200 to 400 milliseconds. The BREAK is used by the operator to interrupt a transmission from the host computer.

ASCII keyboards often have an AUTO LF key. The ASCII code set requires separate codes for carriage return (CR) and line feed (LF) functions. The AUTO LF key, when locked down, causes a line feed code to be transmitted automatically after the carriage return code initiated by the RETURN key. This is convenient when using a terminal in local mode as a typewriter. When operating on-line, the host computer usually recognizes a CR as an end-of-line terminator and echoes back a CR-LF sequence; use of the AUTO LF key in this mode produces double-spaced printing.

Local Control

Some keyboards provide additional keys for initiating local action within the terminal, such as cursor controls (UP, DOWN, LEFT, RIGHT, HOME) for CRT displays. An ON LINE/LOCAL key allows the terminal to be used as an independent typewriter. Other keys display commonly used format "screens" for the entry of designated data items.

Editing Function Keys.   Keyboards in word-processing terminals usually include a cluster of special-purpose keys dedicated to word-processing functions. One may require a word or line deletion; another may ask to open a gap between existing lines on the screen to allow insertion of new material; another may be used to "mark" a group of words to be emphasized during processing. In smart terminals, the editing keys are usually simple switch closures sensed by the terminal logic; they do not generate codes for transmission. In dumb terminals, they generate ASCII control codes that are interpreted by the word-processing program. These functions are discussed in more detail in Chapter 5.

Special-Purpose Keyboards

One class of keyboard has the alphabetic keys arranged in alphabetical order. This is sometimes installed in equipment for use by non-typists—in a warehouse, for example, where inventory clerks enter mainly numeric data with a few very simple messages. Other custom keyboards have special characters and/or layouts.

It is a curious fact that the standard QWERTY keyboard layout, dating from 1873, was designed to slow down typists so that a rising type bar would not prevent the bar for the previous key from falling back into place. The Dvorak Simplified Keyboard (DSK), developed in the 1940s, proved easier to learn and faster to use; DSK users learn touch typing in one-quarter to one-half the time needed by a QWERTY typist, and they commonly reach speeds of 100 words per minute. The DSK never caught on because the typing schools were locked into teaching the standard keyboard, and typewriter manufacturers were reluctant to market a keyboard not taught in the schools.

Now, however, IBM and Smith-Corona both offer the Dvorak key layout at no extra charge, and the scanning encoder makes it very easy to install on computer terminal keyboards. There are many indications that the next 10 years will see a shift of word-processing and clerical services away from a centralized office to terminals and/or small computers in the workers' homes partly for convenience and partly for conservation of energy now used in transportation. The DSK may yet get a chance to show that it can nearly double data entry productivity.

Then there is a class of entry devices which hear little resemblance to traditional keyboards. Many of these are being developed to put microcomputers to work in the service of physically handicapped persons. These entry devices are designed both to compensate for the lost functions and also to make spoken or written communication easier for the handicapped. A sensor that responds to chin movements and initiates microprocessor-controlled operations (such as wheelchair movements or turning the pages of a book) is an example of the first type. Braille keyboards and embossers for the blind are examples of the second type.

3.4 DRIVERS AND BUFFERS

When a keyboard is part of a stand-alone CRT terminal (a unit with CRT, keyboard, display logic, communications interface and power supply in the same housing), the key-pressed strobe and the character code are passed to different sections of the terminal logic: one section displays the character on the screen; the other section serializes the code and transmits it to the host computer. Details of serial interfacing used for this purpose at both ends of the line are given in Chapters 1 and 14.

The computer console display device may consist of a video display module that plugs directly into the computer bus, for which the keyboard is generally a separate package and has its own interfacing logic. The eight keyboard data lines and the strobe line carry signals at standard TTL logic levels, but timing and other considerations preclude direct connection to the computer bus. Instead, communication between the keyboard and the CPU takes place through a simple parallel interface unit such as that shown in Figure 3.10.

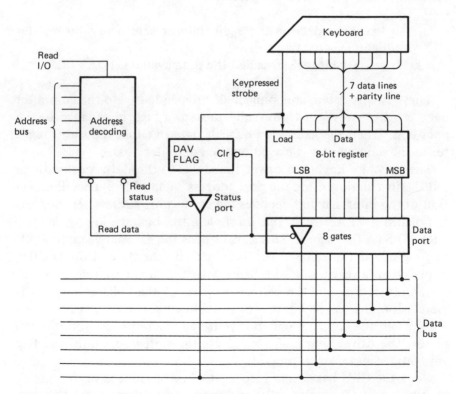

Figure 3.10. Parallel keyboard interface.

This interface unit consists of two separately addressable I/O ports. The status port, shown at the bottom left of the figure, consists of only 1 bit, which determines whether or not a key has been pressed. The data port receives the character code generated by the keyboard.

The series of events by which the computer and a device cooperate and synchronize is called *handshaking*. In effect, the keyboard sets the DAV flag to say "I've got a character for you." The CPU reads the character and resets the flag to indicate "I've taken it." Sometimes the handshaking is carried one stage further in interfaces for faster and more complex I/O devices. The input device interrogates the CPU (saying "Are you sure?"), and only when the CPU has confirmed with yet another signal ("Yes, I'm sure!) does the input device reload the register with a new character.

Let us examine handshaking for the keyboard. When a key is pressed, the keypressed strobe performs two functions:

1. It loads the data on the eight data lines into an 8-bit register which feeds the data port.
2. It sets a 1-bit register called the data available (DAV) flag.

These two registers are connected independently to the computer data bus by gates which normally present a high impedance to the data bus. When the gates are enabled, data in either the status register or the data register is placed on the computer bus.

The software keyboard driver first talks to the status port with an INPUT instruction using the port address. The address decoding section of the interface unit decodes the status port address. If the CPU has placed a READ I/O signal on the control bus, the logic generates a READ STATUS signal. This signal opens the gate between the DAV flag register and one line of the data bus, and the state of the DA flag is placed in a register. If the flag is off, the driver routine takes no action. It returns to the calling program if the calling program is merely looking to see whether or not a key has been pressed. Otherwise, when the calling program is waiting for a response from the operator, the driver continues to address the status port until the flag goes on because a key is pressed.

Once the CPU has determined that a key has indeed been pressed, by finding the DAV flag set, the driver routine reads from the data port by combining the port I/O address with the READ I/O control signal. This time a READ DATA signal is generated that performs two functions:

1. Opens the gates between the data register and the data bus, placing the character code on the data bus and then into the accumulator.
2. Resets the DAV flag to ensure that the same character is not read over and over again.

Extended handshaking is not necessary for a slow, simple device like a keyboard, but it becomes important when communicating with a faster device like a modem, where the CPU may wish to check the parity bit to see that it not only received a character, but received it correctly.

Error Detection

The keyboard circuitry generates a "parity" bit in addition to the 7-bit ASCII or 8-bit EBCDIC character code. This provides a means of checking that the code has been correctly received by the computer. The code generation logic counts the number of 1s in the character, and the parity (most significant) bit of the transmitted character is adjusted to make the total number of 1s even (or odd). For example, the ASCII code for A is 100 00001 binary (41 hex). There are already two 1s in the character, so for even parity the parity bit is zero and 0100 0001 (41 hex) is sent. The code for C is 100 0011 (43 hex) which has three 1s, so the parity bit is 1 and 1100 0011 ((3hex) is sent. The number of 1s received is counted; if even parity is expected and an odd number of ones is received, this indicates a transmission error. Details on error detection and correction are given in the chapter on telecommunications (Chapter 14).

Typical Keyboard Driver Routines

Typical I/O flowcharts and 8080 assembly language routines to determine keyboard status and to input a character from the keyboard are shown in Figure 3.11. A separate subroutine is shown for each function, because two conditions may arise:

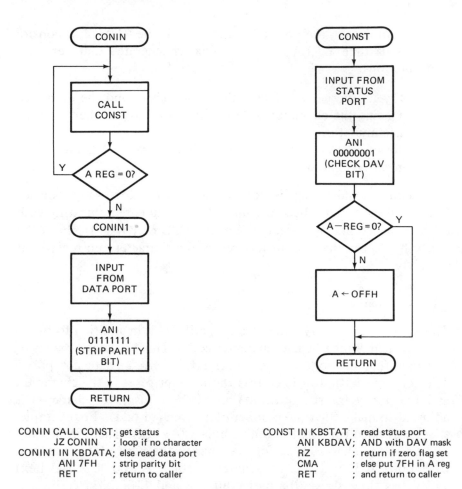

CONIN CALL CONST; get status
      JZ CONIN   ; loop if no character
CONIN1 IN KBDATA; else read data port
      ANI 7FH   ; strip parity bit
      RET   ; return to caller

CONST IN KBSTAT ; read status port
      ANI KBDAV; AND with DAV mask
      RZ   ; return if zero flag set
      CMA   ; else put 7FH in A reg
      RET   ; and return to caller

Figure 3.11.   Programmed console input and status routines.

- A program is performing a repetitive function (such as a dump) which is suspended when a key is pressed.
- A program is waiting for a command from the operator.

In the first case, keyboard status is periodically checked by calling the console status subroutine CONST. If a key is pressed, we return with 7FH in the accumulator and the ZERO condition flag off; the calling program interprets this as a direction to abort the operation. If no key is pressed, we return with zero in the accumulator and with the

ZERO condition flag on, directing the calling program to continue the operation..

In the second case, the main program cannot continue until it gets keyboard input. Calling CONIN establishes a loop that continually calls CONST until a character is available; only then does control pass to CONIN1, which reads the character and returns it to the calling program in the accumulator.

CONIN1 strips off the parity bit (b8) without checking it, which is standard practice in microcomputer console input routines because modern keyboards are so reliable. Generally, a character typed on the keyboard is displayed on the console output device, so that if an error does occur, it can be seen and corrected at once. In many systems the b8 (parity) keyboard output terminal is left unconnected, and the eighth data line carries the keypressed strobe signal, thus saving one conductor.

4
The Video Display Terminal

4.1 DISPLAY PRESENTATION PRINCIPLES

A video display module is an output device which processes data from the computer to be displayed on a cathode ray tube (CRT) such as that used in a television set. In fact, personal computer systems sometimes use a TV set to display output, linking the computer to it with a small RF (radio frequency) modulator tuned to an unused TV channel. More often, however, the display device is a video monitor, a unit containing a CRT tube, video circuits and power supplies but no RF or sound circuitry, as shown in Figure 4.1. The video display module is the interface between the computer and the display. It converts digital data into video signals.

In this chapter we discuss only modules for presenting alphanumeric data. Modules for presenting pictorial data have somewhat different requirements. They are discussed in Chapter 8. However, these alphanumeric display units can also be used for *low-resolution graphics* —that is, pictures drawn with ordinary alphabetic characters or symbols or with special shapes generated in the same manner as the alphabet. Individuals who use their computers only for computation or word processing may not be interested in knowing how characters are built on the screen. But for those who want to create designs or graphic enhancements to games, using home computers such as the Apple, Atari, Sorcerer and others, knowledge of the capabilities and restrictions of the display generator is essential.

Figure 4.1.   Typical 15-inch and 9-inch video monitors.

Raster Generation

A raster is a pattern of horizontal lines drawn successively from top to bottom of a television or CRT screen. A sawtooth voltage is applied to the horizontal deflection circuits of the CRT so that the beam moves at even speed from left to right across the screen. When the beam reaches the extreme right of the screen, the short retrace portion of the waveform returns it rapidly to the left. During this retrace period a blanking voltage is applied to the beam generator so that the bright spot on the screen is suppressed and invisible.

A similar, slower, sawtooth voltage is applied to the vertical deflection circuits, so that each horizontal line is a little below the previous one. When the beam reaches the bottom right of the screen, vertical as well as horizontal retrace occurs, and the beam is returned to the top left of the screen (Figure 4.2). The beam is blanked for the whole of the vertical retrace time, as well as during each horizontal retrace. The set of horizontal lines produced during each vertical scan is called a field.

On a TV screen, the raster is always visible; the picture is generated by varying the beam intensity during the scan. Thus, different parts of the screen vary from full brilliance down to black in many steps.

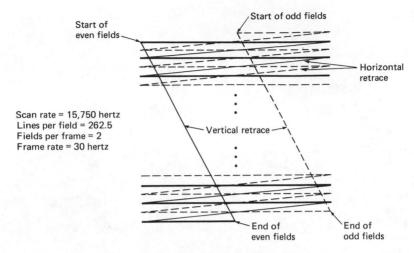

Start of
even fields

Start of odd fields

Horizontal
retrace

Scan rate = 15,750 hertz
Lines per field = 262.5
Fields per frame = 2
Frame rate = 30 hertz

Vertical retrace

End of
even fields

End of
odd fields

Figure 4.2. Interlaced raster.

Computer terminal screens also generate a raster in the same way; however, the screen is normally dark and is driven to full brightness only when a part of a letter or number is being formed.

Alphanumeric displays generally use short-persistence CRT's with TV raster scanning, using the TV horizontal scan frequency (15,750 hertz). The 525-line scan that is standard in TV sets is obtained by using 262.5 lines for each field, but interlacing the scan lines of alternate fields to give the appearance of closer lines and thus of sharper detail in the picture (Figure 4.2). Thirty complete frames per second are displayed with two fields per frame.

Alphanumeric displays do not display so much detail, and interlacing is seldom used. Instead, the synchronizing signals supplied by the video module create a raster with 262 lines for a complete frame (of only one field). Thus, the frame rate goes up to 60 per second (Figure 4.3).

Not all the raster is usable without complicated and expensive circuitry. The beam deflection rate is nonlinear near the ends of its travel, both vertically and horizontally, and results in distortion at the outer edges of the raster. Letters near the edges become skinnier or fatter than elsewhere, or are slanted. The amplitude of the scan is therefore adjusted so that the raster is larger than the screen, and the beam is not turned on until it enters the linear portion. The entire screen area can now be used for display, since the nonlinear portions of the raster are not visible and contain no information. As a result, only 240 of the 262 scan lines of the noninterlaced raster are usable. At the normal horizontal scan rate of 15,750 hertz, the usable portion of each scan line lasts for 64 microseconds. These numbers become important when the timing for a video display module is considered.

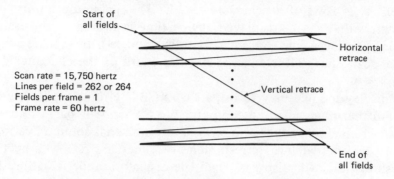

Figure 4.3. Noninterlaced raster.

Throughout this chapter, line refers to a single horizontal scan line used to make part of each letter, and row refers to a group of scan lines of sufficient number to display a row of characters plus adequate vertical separation from the next row for readability. The number of characters displayable in a row depends upon the bandwidth of the circuit and the granularity of the monitor. Some constraint is also imposed by the access time of the character-generator read-only memory (CG ROM). Better displays are hence more expensive. With the common bandwidth of 12 megahertz, 80 characters per row is no problem.

Refresh Memory

Alphanumeric characters sent by the computer to the display module are loaded into successive locations of a block of memory, a hardware buffer that is part of the module. This memory is usually 8 bits wide to accommodate 8-bit ASCII code. Memory length depends upon how many characters are to be displayed on the screen as well as upon whether additional memory is required for editing purposes or for I/O buffering.

The portion of the memory containing the characters currently displayed, called refresh memory, is accessed once per frame (i.e., 60 times per second) to refresh the display. If this were not done, the characters would disappear within a few milliseconds because of the low persistence of the phosphor of a CRT. Refresh memory is usually 2,048 (2K) bytes long and stores 1,960 characters, displayed on the screen as 24 rows of 80 characters each. The maximum number of characters that can be displayed at one time is limited by the usable width of the scan line (64 microseconds standard), the usable number of scan lines (240 standard) and the width of the character dot matrix.

A display module may form part of a CRT terminal, or it may be a board that plugs into the computer bus. When it is part of an external terminal, characters are sent to it via a serial communications link to be entered into refresh memory. They are retrieved by the refresh circuitry for display. When the display module is within the host computer, refresh memory is physically located on the display module but is functionally part of main memory. Characters are stored

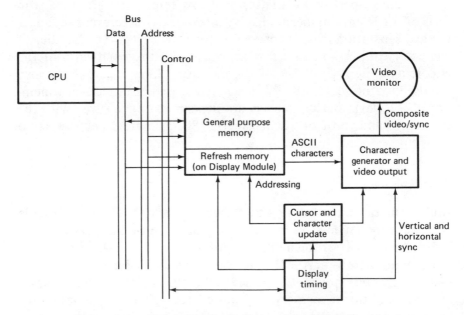

Figure 4.4. Alphanumeric display module; block diagram.

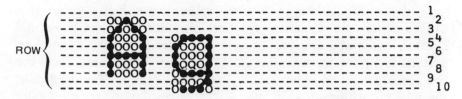

Each character row has 10 scan lines, of which
#1 is blank for interrow spacing.

Figure 4.5.   (A) Character generation on 5 X 7 dot matrix.

there by the CPU via the address and data buses, using standard memory reference instructions from the CPU's instruction set. However, refresh memory is accessible to the CPU only during horizontal and vertical retrace periods. The locations occupied by refresh memory are not available for program or data storage. A block diagram of a typical display module of this type is shown in Figure 4.4.

Individual Character Generation

Each character displayed is constructed on the screen by a dot pattern contained within a rectangular array as shown in Figure 4.5A. Common matrix sizes are:

- 5 wide by 7 high (relatively coarse).
- 7 wide by 9 high (good readability—can generate special type fonts including Greek, Cyrillic and the Japanese Katakana).
- 9 wide by 13 high (high quality—usable for phototypesetting).

All the dot arrays required for constructing a complete displayable character set are contained in a read-only memory called the character generator. Figure 4.5B shows the 128 arrays of dots, together with the codes in binary and hexadecimal, for the standard ASCII character set. To display an A at some screen position, the ASCII code (hex 41) is obtained from the proper location in refresh memory. The code is applied to the seven high-order address lines of the character generator (Figure 4.6). The three low-order address bits are supplied by the scan-line counter, which keeps track of which scan line in the row is currently active. The horizontal pattern of five 0s and 1s found here in the CG ROM is loaded in parallel into a shift register. It is shifted out to the screen in synchronism with the beam travel and controls the spot intensity: a bright dot appears for each 1 in the bit pattern and none for a 0. For an A, the same seven locations in the character generator are accessed by successive scan lines, regareless of the screen position at which the A is to be displayed. We show later how screen position is determined.

Figure 4.5. (B) Typical ASCII character set on 5 X 7 dot matrix.

The 240 available scan lines allow 24 rows of 10 scan lines each, for both upper- and lowercase characters. The lowercase characters (g, j, p, q and y) with descenders—portions of the character which descend below the line— do not require a larger matrix; they are still constructed with a 5 X 7 matrix, but the topmost dot pattern for the letter is not accessed until the fourth scan line is in process. The ASCII codes for these five letters activate special circuitry which subtracts 2 from the value in the scan line counter before applying it to the CG ROM address lines. Hence a pattern accessed by a count of, say 3, is not accessed until the actual line count reaches 3 + 2 = 5. If the display is restricted to uppercase letters (where descenders are not

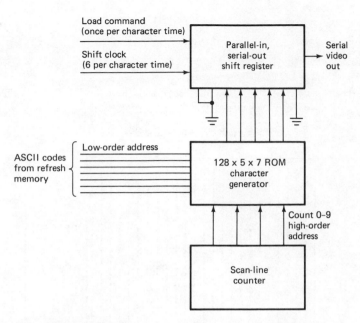

Figure 4.6.   Character generator; block diagram.

required), the characters occupy only eight scan lines, and thus 30 rows of characters can be displayed.

Display Building

We now discuss the manner in which a screen of characters is built up.

Screen Geometry.   Refer to Figure 4.7, which shows the scanning sequence of a complete screen containing 24 rows of 80 characters each. The column positions in each row are numbered 0 through 79; the row positions are numbered 0 through 23. Each row uses 10 scan lines, for a total of 240 live scan lines. (A live line is one actually used for display.) There are 262 lines for the screen, but the first 11 and last 11 are not usable because of nonlinearity in the CRT vertical deflection circuits. In the same way, horizontal nonlinearity forbids the use of the entire width of a scan line. The proportion of usable to dead space on the screen varies from about two-thirds for an unmodified TV set to about nine-tenths for a high-quality video monitor.

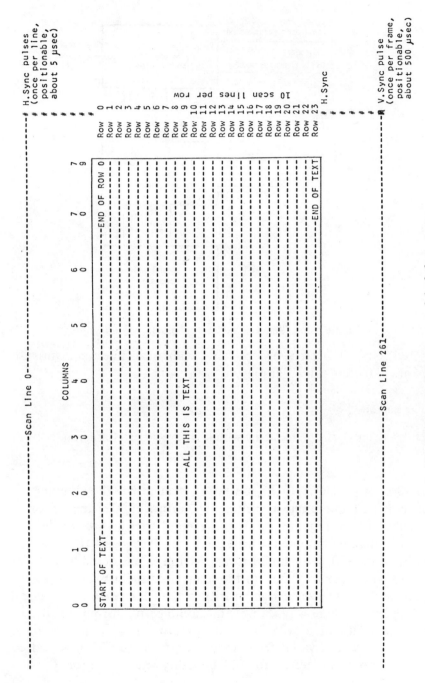

Figure 4.7.   Building a screenful of characters.

Screen Timing. To obtain a stable display, the frame repetition rate is locked to the 60-hertz supply frequency. For compatibility with TV standards, the horizontal oscillator frequency is a nominal 15,720 hertz, giving 262 scan lines per frame. The duration of a frame is 1/60 second or 16-2/3 milliseconds; a scan line is 16-2/3 milliseconds/ 262 = 63.6 microseconds. If we assume that 88 percent of this time is usable for display, we have 56 microseconds for 80 characters, or 700 nanoseconds for each pattern of six dots (including one dot for intercharacter spacing) for each character. This is 700 nanoseconds/ 16 = 117 nanoseconds per dot. The video dot clock frequency is about 9 megahertz; the exact rate is adjusted to give good character proportions. Figure 4.8 shows the effect of increasing and decreasing the video dot clock frequency for a fixed character rate. Later in the chapter we describe how the various timing signals are generated.

(A) Slow video clock — wide characters.

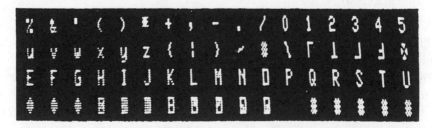

(B) Fast video clock — compressed characters.

Figure 4.8. Effect of varying video clock for fixed character rate.

Row Generation.   Refer once more to Figure 4.7. Each of the 24 X 80 = 1960 character positions on the live area of the screen corresponds to one location in refresh memory. To build a row of characters, we do the following:

- Scan line 0. Interrow spacing. Address the 80 refresh memory locations of the current row successively, but do not turn on the beam.
- Scan lines 1 and 2. Address the 80 memory locations of the current row successively. For each character, address the character generator, using the line count for the high-order address bits and the ASCII code found in refresh memory for the low-order bits. Decode the character; if it has a descender, put five 0s in the shift register; otherwise put in the dot pattern obtained from the character generator. Shift out the contents of the shift register to the intensity control circuits to turn the beam on for a 1 or off for a 0.
- Scan lines 3 to 7. Address the 80 memory locations of the current row successively. For each character, obtain the dot pattern as described above, put the pattern in the shift register and shift it out to the intensity control.
- Scan lines 8 and 9. Address the 80 memory locations of the current row successively. Decode each character; if it has a descender, obtain the dot pattern from the character generator and shift it out to the display; otherwise turn off the beam for one character time. After processing the eightieth memory location, advance the row counter by 1 count to address the next 80 locations of refresh memory.

This sequence continues until all 24 rows have been built. Blanking circuits then turn off the beam for the last (dead) 11 scan lines (251 through 261), and a vertical sync pulse is generated at the end of line 261.

An empty character position on the screen is produced only if the corresponding location in refresh memory contains an ASCII space code (hex 20). Hex 00 is a valid ASCII code (NUL) and is displayable, usually as a square, although other patterns are also found.

Frequency References

The display system clock is a tightly controlled reference frequency from which all other timing signals are derived. It can be either the video dot clock, emitting one pulse for each dot position, or the character clock, emitting one pulse for each set of dots belonging to one character. For a matrix there are six dots horizontally; the dot rate is therefore six times the character rate. There are two advantages to using the character clock:

- It is easier to lock it to the supply frequency; the character rate is about 1.25 megahertz, whereas the video rate is about 9 megahertz.
- It allows adjustment of the dot rate for optimum character shape (see Figure 4.8).

The simplified block diagram of Figure 4.9 shows one method of obtaining the character clock and related timing signals. Many other methods are possible, of course.

The phase-locked loop (PLL) consists of a voltage-controlled oscillator (VCO) and a phase detector. In the absence of signals at the EXT REF and INT REF terminals, the VCO oscillates at approxi-

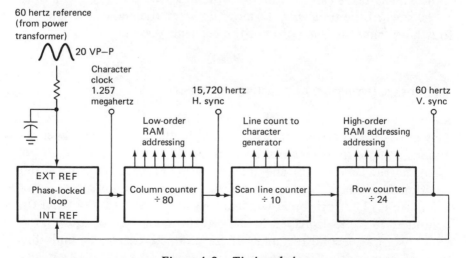

Figure 4.9.   Timing chain.

mately 1.152 megahertz. From this squarewave output a narrow character clock pulse is derived that loads the video shift register with the dot pattern supplied by the character generator. The character clock is divided by 80 in the column counter to generate the horizontal sync frequency of 15,720 hertz; variable delay circuits (not shown) allow fine control of sync pulse generation to position the display on the screen. The outputs of the column counter address the same 80 locations in refresh memory for each of 10 scan lines; the pulse emitted by the line counter after the tenth line advances the row counter and causes the column counter to address the next block of 80 refresh memory locations.

The pulse repetition rate at the output of the row counter is $1,152,000/(80 \times 10 \times 24) = 60$ hertz. This signal is fed back to the INT REF terminal of the PLL; a 60-hertz, 20-volt peak-to-peak signal obtained directly from the power transformer is applied to the EXT REF terminal of the PLL, where it is clipped and squared. The phase detector of the PLL compares the phases of the external reference and the divided VCO signal. If the divided VCO signal leads the supply, the phase detector generates an error signal to reduce VCO frequency. If the divided VCO signal lags the supply, the error signal increases VCO frequency. Thus, the timing signal chain is locked to the supply frequency to stabilize the display. Additional circuitry (not shown) takes care of the insertion and blanking of 11 scan lines at the start of the frame and 11 more between the end of the twenty-fourth row and the generation of the vertical sync pulse.

4.2 SCREEN UPDATING AND CURSOR CONTROL

So far, we have considered the mechanism for displaying characters that are now in refresh memory. How do they get there? Each location in the refresh memory corresponds to a unique character position on the screen. The character corresponding to the code in this location is displayed at the character position on the screen every frame time. The position at which a new character received from the computer is to be displayed is marked on the screen by the *cursor,* which is either a solid rectangle of full character size or an underline of character width displayed in the otherwise blank separation scan line. The cursor may be steady or blinking.

The character input and cursor display circuits perform the following functions:

- When a character arrives from the computer, enter it into fresh memory at the location corresponding to the current cursor position and then move the cursor to the next character position on the screen.
- Upon reaching the end of one row, move the cursor to the start of the next row.
- Move the cursor directly to the top left (HOME) position on the screen under manual or software control.
- Move the cursor left or right, one character position at a time, under manual or software control.
- Move the cursor up or down, one row at a time, under manual or software control.

Cursors sometimes act as markers for the following optional functions:

- Erase from the cursor position to the end of the row.
- Erase from the cursor position to the end of the screen.
- Transmit to the CPU all characters from the cursor position to the end of the screen.
- Mark the beginning and end of a character string that is to be emphasized or protected.
- *Scroll*—that is, the cursor remains in the bottom row of the screen. All characters received are entered there. When the end of the row is reached or a carriage return is received, the screen is scrolled—each line is moved up one position. In other words:
  - Move out the present top line.
  - Move each remaining line up one position.
    - *line 2 to line 1
    - *line 3 to line 2
    - * . . . .
    - *line 24 to line 23
  - The bottom line now becomes empty and the cursor is reset to its beginning, where characters start to be recorded.

There are many methods of displaying the cursor and updating the refresh memory. The easiest method to understand, though it is complex in detail, is the count-and-compare method, for which Figure 4.10 is a simplified block diagram.

A character received from the CPU waits in a character buffer until the UPDATE signal occurs. This gates the character into the refresh memory. The location at which to enter the character is determined by the present cursor position. This is found by comparing the display counter and the cursor counter, and generating UPDATE when they coincide. In each counter, the low-order bits count character positions within a row; the high-order bits count rows on the screen.

The display counter is driven continuously by the character clock. It is reset by the vertical sync pulse at the start of a frame to address the first location of the refresh memory (home). The column counter advances at the end of every character time. Thus, after homing, the codes contained in successive memory locations of row 1 are applied to the character generator (Figure 4.6). The column counter is reset by each horizontal sync pulse, so that locations 1 through 80 are addressed by each scan line in the row, while characters are built up. Overflow of the column counter is gated with overflow of the scan line counter to advance the row counter. This procedure continues until all 24 rows of characters and spaces have been built on the screen.

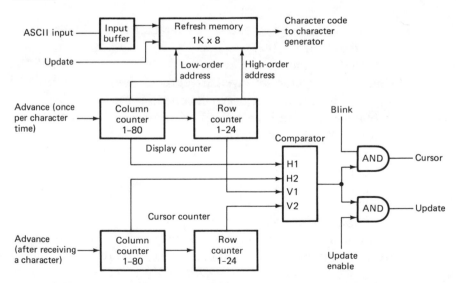

Figure 4.10. Count-and-compare cursor control; block diagram.

The cursor counter is static until a character arrives at the input register; it is advanced by the signal which loads this character from the input register into refresh memory. The cursor counter is constantly compared to the display counter, which is counting continuously. When they coincide, the comparator produces an equal output and gates the square or underline signal with a *blink* signal to generate a cursor at that character position. Coincidence occurs for every scan line of the row to which the cursor row counter points. Since the cursor gate passes a signal at every coincidence, a "solid" rectangle is built on the screen. An alternative is to pass the cursor signal only during scan line 10 of this row to create an underline. When blink is provided, it is usually set for a 1-second period, so that the cursor is on the 30 frames and then off for the next 30 frames.

When a character code arrives in the input buffer, the data available signal cuases generation of the UPDATE ENABLE (Figure 4.10). When the display and cursor counters coincide, UPDATE is produced and the character code is loaded from the input buffer into this location in the refresh memory. Thereafter it is displayed on the screen. Upon completion of the load, UPDATE ENABLE becomes inactive and advances the cursor column counter. When the cursor column counter overflows, it resets to zero and advances the cursor row counter to push the cursor to the start of the next row.

The cursor may be moved to any position on the screen without changing the characters displayed. This is done by sending a special ASCII code to change the value in one of the counters. The RIGHT code adds one to the column counter, and the LEFT code subtracts one. The DOWN code adds one to the row counter, and the UP code subtracts one. Some terminals allow the cursor to be moved directly to a specified position by sending the sequence ESC-XY, where ESC is the ASCII escape code, = is the code for that symbol, X is a character whose hex value represents the column number (in the range 0 to 132 decimal, or 0 to 84 hex), and Y is a character whose hex value represents the row number (in the range 0 to 23 decimal, or 0 to 17 hex). The hex value of the first character is forced into the column counter, and the hex value of the second character is forced into the row counter. Thus, if we sent ESC=m*, the cursor would move directly to column 51 in row 11. The codes are usually chosen so that the space (hex 20) represents a counter value of 0 (row or column number 1). The HOME key or a corresponding ASCII code resets both cursor counters simultaneously, moving the cursor to the top left corner of the screen.

By use of these basic cursor movement facilities, other circuitry can "mark" one or more character strings on the display by setting the eighth bit of every character within the string to be set apart; these marked characters can then be emphasized or moved to other locations for editing purposes.

Display units that are integrated into the computer can be much more flexible in their updating methods. Here a portion of main memory performs the functions of refresh memory and is hence directly addressable by the CPU. (It is still referred to here as refresh memory.) Scanning and accessing characters for display uses the same hardware timing technique. Cursor control and refresh memory updating can be done with software, to provide such features as:

- Double-column displays (Figure 4.11). These are used in word-processing or phototypesetting systems.
- Command input areas. A command input area consists of one or two rows (usually at the bottom of the screen) reserved for the entry and display of prompts and replies without disturbing text in the data area above. Commands sometimes appear in reversed video. If normal video is bright on a dark background, reversed video is dark on a bright background.
- Multiple windows and split screen. These are screen areas of various sizes and shapes containing data independently updated from different sources. They are useful in instrumentation displays, especially when a different color can be used for each window. Double column is one form of split screen. The screen may also be divided horizontally, with text in the top half coming from one file and text in the bottom half from another. This is useful in comparing files or for browsing through a file of compiler error messages (displayed at the top) while making corrections in the source code (displayed at the bottom).

The contents of the refresh memory do not have to be updated at a particular instant but can be updated during the vertical retrace time. Even when a software driver is taking care of cursor movements, scrol-

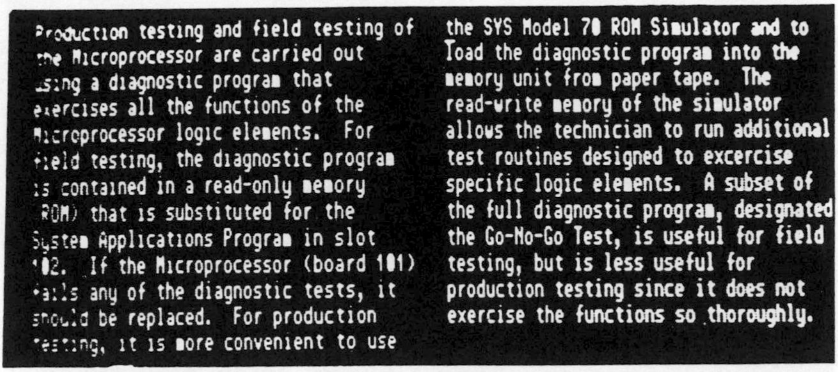

Production testing and field testing of the SYS Model 70 ROM Simulator and to the Microprocessor are carried out load the diagnostic program into the using a diagnostic program that memory unit from paper tape. The exercises all the functions of the read-write memory of the simulator Microprocessor logic elements. For allows the technician to run additional field testing, the diagnostic program test routines designed to excercise is contained in a read-only memory specific logic elements. A subset of ROM) that is substituted for the the full diagnostic program, designated System Applications Program in slot the Go-No-Go Test, is useful for field 02. If the Microprocessor (board 101) testing, but is less useful for fails any of the diagnostic tests, it production testing since it does not should be replaced. For production exercise the functions so thoroughly. testing, it is more convenient to use

Figure 4.11. Part of a double column display.

ling and updating, the entire screen can be changed in a few seconds. If a new screen of data is prepared and stored elsewhere in memory and is then transferred to the refresh memory at a very high rate during vertical retrace by direct memory access (DMA) methods, the change of data appears instantantaneous.

4.3 DISPLAY TIMING

The basic display timing formulas are:

1. Vertical scan rate = 60 hertz
2. Horizontal scan rate = 6 (R * S + B), where
    R is the number of character rows.
    S is the number of scan lines per character.
    B is the number of blanked scan lines (for separation or outside the display areas).
3. Horizontal character rate = (H * C)/L, where
    H is the horizontal scan rate.
    C is the number of characters per row.
    L is the number of live scan lines (in the display area).
4. Dot rate = 0.5(H * (D + U), where
    H is the horizontal scan rate.
    D is the number of dots per character width.
    U is the number of undots used for intercharacter separation.

There are some definite constraints on these rates.

- The vertical scan rate is the same as the supply frequency; it is phase-synchronized to the supply to ensure a stable display.
- The live vertical scan time is less than the full scan time to reduce distortion.
- The live horizontal scan time is less than the full horizontal scan time to reduce distortion.
- The video rate is approximately half the maximum dot frequency, including undots between characters.

For unmodified TV sets, the usable display area is approximately two-thirds of the full frame. In custom-designed (and correspondingly more expensive) monitors, the usable area approaches nine-tenths of the frame.

The dot rate is limited by the bandwidth of the device. For black and white TV sets the bandwidth is seldom more than 3.5 megahertz; but for high-quality monitors, it is 20 megahertz or more.

These limitations restrict a readable display to 32 characters per row if the video is transferred to a TV set via an RF modulator, or to 64 characters if the display module is directly connected to the video input of a TV set or an inexpensive monitor. A 12-megahertz monitor can display 80 characters per row. Displays of 85 to 132 characters require a bandwidth of 20 megahertz or so and special circuitry to access characters fast enough from the refresh memory; several intermediate character buffers may be needed to ensure that a character is always ready when needed.

5
Terminals

5.1 DEFINITIONS

A remote terminal is equipment that communicates with a host computer over a line. A *dumb terminal* consists of a keyboard, a display device (CRT or printer), a bidirectional communication interface and power supplies. It sends and displays one character at a time. A microcomputer system sometimes acts as a dumb terminal if the user wishes merely to have the services of a larger installation on a datanet in conversational mode, without transferring executable program files in either direction.

A *smart terminal* has built-in editing features and a control program that allows a full screen of data to be transferred or displayed as a unit. This program handles the transmission protocol — that is, the procedure for sending and receiving blocks of data and checking them for transmission errors.

An *intelligent terminal* is usually a microcomputer system with external storage and sometimes a printer. The control program allows data to be entered in disk files off-line, or local programs to be executed. The software and hardware concerned with communication often allow the terminal to answer a call from a host computer, transfer disk files in either direction and disconnect on completion of the transfers, all without operator intervention.

5.2 DUMB TERMINALS

In a stand-alone microcomputer system, a dumb CRT terminal which behaves like a Teletype is most commonly used as the console. A typical CRT terminal has an RS-232C communication interface capable of operating at 9600 bits per second. For hard copy, the system includes either a keyboard/printer terminal, which can also be used as an alternate console, or a read-only printer. For high throughput, and to allow the more sophisticated features of the device to be implemented, the hard-copy device has an internal storage buffer for 256 or more characters and a communications interface operating at 1200 bits per second or more, even though the printing rate is usually slower than this.

The console is unsophisticated. It is character-oriented, that is, each keystroke is transmitted to the microcomputer, which echos it to the display device. The microcomputer accumulates characters in an input buffer until a carriage return (CR) code is received. The operating system or application program then processes the entire line.

Current 8-bit microcomputer operating systems, editors and other utilities do not support the "page entry" mode, in which 20 or more lines of text can be entered and edited on the screen and then transmitted from the console as a block. Instead, text manipulation is performed by an editor utility, as the result of commands received from the keyboard. These commands consist of ASCII codes transmitted in the normal manner; they may be single control characters generated by special function keys, or printable characters which have special meanings to the editor when an editing mode is entered. In the same way, the editor controls the position of the cursor on the screen by sending control codes to the terminal.

All editing sophistication is in the microcomputer program, not in the terminal itself. In fact, the simpler the terminal, the easier it is to integrate it into a general-purpose microcomputer system. The essential features to look for, when choosing a terminal, are:

- Is transmission speed switch-selectable for the standard rates between 300 and 9600 bits per second?
- Is parity generation and checking switch-selectable for even or odd, or parity bit always 0, or parity bit always 1?
- Does it provide full-duplex mode? Here, keyed characters are displayed only when echoed by the microcomputer. Most terminals provide full half duplex switching as a standard feature.

- Does the main keyboard have a *full* set of 96 printable ASCII characters? Many editor programs and some compilers require, in addition to parentheses, brackets, braces, the commercial "at", and the vertical (i.e., [ ], { , } , @, |), which are not found on EBCDIC and Teletype keyboards.
- Are special function keys programmable by the user?

Typical video display terminals which provide all or most of these features, priced at around $1,000, are the Lear-Siegler ADM3A, the Hazeltine 1500, and the Soroc 120. Printing terminals, such as the Texas Instruments Silent 700 series, or the Teletype 43 are also dumb terminals suitable for console use, but they cost a few hundred dollars more than the video terminals.

5.3 SMART TERMINALS

A smart terminal is primarily a page-oriented CRT device. Characters are displayed on the screen as they are keyed but not transmitted individually to the host computer. Both the display logic and the communications interface are more sophisticated than those of dumb terminals, although a dumb terminal mode is usually provided. Prices range from $1,500 to $2,500 or more, depending on the facilities provided. A smart terminal is generally considered overkill for the dedicated console of a microcomputer system. However, if the user also requires access to a large mainframe that supports page mode data entry and high-speed synchronous communication protocol, switching a smart terminal from one type of service to the other, as needed, saves the cost of an additional terminal.

Refresh memory generally holds more than one full screen of characters; it may be up to 132 characters wide and 50 lines deep. If the screen cannot accommodate all of these 6,600 characters at one time, both vertical and horizontal scrolling are provided so that the entire refresh memory may be examined and modified. Horizontal scrolling allows either the first 80 columns or the last 80 columns of the text on the screen to be displayed, with some overlap between the two halves, UP, DOWN, LEFT, RIGHT, and HOME cursor keys are provided to allow nondestructive cursor movement to any point on the screen. In addition, function keys provide insertion of new material into text already on the screen and movement or deletion of blocks of text between markers. Word wraparound is often provided: a word that does not fit completely at the end of one text line is automatically pushed down to the start of the next line. When the user has edited the text to his satisfaction, he presses an ENTER key (sometimes labeled TRANSMIT) to send a block of text to the computer. The action of this key varies from terminal to terminal; sometimes the entire contents of refresh memory are transmitted, but more often only text from the cursor position to the end of the screen is sent.

The communications interface of a smart terminal is programmed for the line protocol demanded by the host computer. When the ENTER key is pressed, the text is not sent all at once but in blocks. Maximum block length is specified by the protocol in use. Each block includes check bytes that allow the host to determine whether or not there were any transmission errors; if there were, the host requests retransmission of that block. Some of the line protocols in common use are described in more detail in Chapter 14. It is enough to say here that a smart terminal handles only the line protocol installed at the time of ordering. It may be inherently capable of handling other protocols, but to install them requires replacement of the ROM containing the microprocessor program.

Some smart terminals have interface hardware and software routines for a printer. This is useful when you want to print selected portions of text received from the host; pressing a PRINT key sends some or all of the text in the refresh memory to a local printer.

5.4 INTELLIGENT TERMINALS

An intelligent terminal is a complete microcomputer system that has external storage and may have other peripherals, such as a printer and/or interfaces for capturing analog data in real time. The software contains sophisticated telecommunication routines that allow an unattended terminal to answer a telephone call from a host computer, transfer data or program files in either direction and disconnect itself from the line when all transfers are complete. Other software allows an operator to load and run programs resident on the local disk drives.

Almost any general-purpose microcomputer system can be used as an intelligent terminal to communicate both with large mainframes and with other microcomputers. As of April, 1981, several hundred privately owned Bulletin Board Systems were listed across the country, many of them available free to personal computer owners 24 hours per day for notices, messages and software exchange. Microcomputer software in the public domain has also allowed any microcomputer system to become an intelligent terminal with access to large data bases on time-sharing systems such as The Source at moderate cost.

5.5 CLUSTERS

A cluster is a computer system connecting multiple work stations to a larger host computer over a single communications line. It is economical because the expensive items, such as a high-capacity hard disk drive and a letter-quality printer are shared among several inexpensive dumb terminals. A multiuser operating system allows each work station access to sophisticated word-processing programs and queues the output from these in disk files for printing or transmission to the mainframe host computer. The cluster disk space can be used efficiently, since only programs that are in constant use need be permanently resident on the cluster disk. Large programs that are used only occasionally can be stored in the host's disk space and downloaded to the cluster over the communication line when needed.

The number of work stations that can be supported by a multiuser system is limited by the speed of the computer and the amount of work it has to do to satisfy the users. Each additional user adds to the load and thus increases the time a user has to wait for a response to a command. A cluster can support more users without degradation of the response time, because major functions can be assigned to separate microprocessors that share some of the resources. For example, one may handle all input from and output to the work stations via memory buffers; another may handle file management; and a third may handle communication with the mainframe host via disk queues and/or spooling of word processor output to the printer.

Eight-bit microprocessors are limited in their processing power and thus have not been considered suitable for cluster systems, but as the powerful new 16-bit micros (8086, Z8000, 68000) come into full production and supporting software is developed, we may expect to see them replacing minicomputers in this type of environment.

6
Printers and Printing Terminals

6.1 INTRODUCTION

Printing terminals consist of a package containing:

- Keyboard.
- Printer.
- Communications interface.
- Sometimes a built-in acoustic coupler.
- Power supplies for all the above.

Complete terminals of this kind vary from small portable units with an 80-column printer, weighing 30 to 40 pounds, to large units with a 132-column impact printer, often built into a stand or desk and weighing 100 to 150 pounds. Functionally, they can all serve either as remote terminals communicating with a host computer over a telephone line or as the local console device for a microcomputer.

Printer speed may limit the usefulness of a printing terminal as a console device and may complicate text editing to build documents or source language programs. For this reason, it is often more convenient to have either a serial CRT terminal or a memory-mapped video display module and keyboard as the console device, and to generate hard copy on a read-only printer. Printers are usually equipped with a communications interface and a memory buffer to hold 132 or 256 characters. For local use they may lack these options and be connected through a multiconductor cable to a parallel interface board in the microcomputer.

Speed Versus Type Quality

Printer choice considers the tradeoffs between speed, type quality and price, and such a choice is seldom easy. A printer with quality comparable to an office Selectric is slow and expensive. Diablo, Qume and NEC printers use embossed characters, have a choice of type faces, have a top speed of 30 to 60 characters per second and cost $2,000 to $3,000.

Printing speeds of up to 120 characters per second are available on band printers; few typefaces are available; and changing the band takes a longer time than does changing a golf ball or daisy wheel. Prices range between $3,000 and $6,000. The type is clean and sharp and provides good-looking reports, but none of the typefaces would be anyone's first choice for correspondence or brochures.

A dot-matrix printer is likely to be the choice for speeds up to 900 characters per second or when low price is the primary consideration. Several machines in the $550 to $1,200 price range have dot matrices that write lowercase characters with true descenders, (i.e., the tails of g, j, p, q and y descent below the line) and print at speeds up to 165 characters per second. But however readable the typeface, it is obviously a dot matrix. This is fine for system statistics and any kind of management report that would be acceptable on the green-and-white paper that comes out of large systems at 1,200 lines per minute from the chain printer. But the typeface is not acceptable in any document that would normally be typed on the best bond paper.

Even in the dot-matrix printers, speed has its price. Machines that print at 300 to 900 characters per second are also in the $3,000 to $5,000 price range. However, some of the machines in this class allow high quality to be obtained at the expense of speed, under program control. At high speed, the carriage makes only a single pass over each line. But for better print quality, the carriage makes two, three, or even four passes over the line with a very slight displacement each time. Thus, each character is made up of more dots with closer spacing, and even curved portions of the character are smoothed out. One such machine not only uses extremely small dots but also stores several complete typefaces in a special character generator read-only memory. The multipass printing of this machine cannot be distinguished from that of a phototypesetter or a good typewriter without a magnifying glass.

Low-Speed Printers

Printers which have a printing speed between 10 and 60 characters per second are classified as low-speed printers. In this group we find:

- Teletype models 33 and 35.
- IBM I/O Selectric typewriters.
- Daisy-wheel printers (Diablo Hytype I and II, Qume and NEC Spinwriter.

We now examine in more detail the characteristics of these printers.

6.2 TELETYPE MODELS 33 and 35

Although largely superseded by more modern terminals, so many thousands of these workhorses are still in the field that they cannot be ignored. They are to be found in RO, KSR (keyboard send/receive), and ASR (automatic send/receive) versions.

The Teletype models 33 and 35 (an enhanced, rugged brother of the 33) are cylinder printers. That is, the type characters are embossed on a cylinder (Figure 6.1) that is mounted on a vertical shaft. The cylinder both rotates around and moves vertically along its axis to bring the desired character into the printing position. A hammer drives the cylinder sharply toward the platen so that the character strikes the paper through the ribbon.

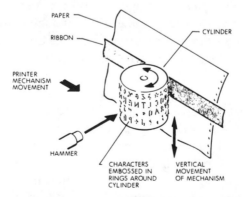

Figure 6.1.   Teletype print mechanism; simplified diagram.

The Teletype is a serial device. The electronics accept a serial bit stream from the line, convert it to parallel format and use the bit pattern to drive solenoids which, through mechanical linkages, lift and rotate the cylinder to bring the character into the print position.

The 8-bit ASCII code set is used, with one leading start bit and two trailing stop bits. The early models required what is known as a current loop (either 20 milliamperes or 60 milliamperes): The principal interface between the line and the shift register is a relay which requires a current flow of 20 to 60 milliamperes to energize it properly. For a long line which has more internal resistance, a higher voltage is needed to provide the required current through the loop, which is a disadvantage when connecting cable length varies.

Later models are optionally fitted with an RS-232 converter which accepts bipolar signals in the range ±3 to ±25 volts, and generates zero current or 20 milliamperes to drive the relay.

The printing speed is only 10 characters per second, and the machines are noisy. They are cheap and sturdy console devices. The ASR (automatic send/receive) models are fitted with a reliable paper-tape punch and a paper-tape reader with mechanical sensing fingers, both driven from one main printer motor.

The machine operates in full duplex. A three-wire connection (keyboard send, printer receive and common ground) allows characters typed on the keyboard to be echoed back by the host computer, thereby providing an indication that the communications link is working correctly.

6.3 SELECTRIC I/O TYPEWRITERS

The I/O Selectric™ typewriter was the first terminal to provide both upper- and lowercase characters and an increased printing speed (14.9 characters per second. Although there are still many machines in the field, the Selectric has been superseded by newer printers that are faster and more reliable. Various models of I/O Selectric are used as computer console devices for some IBM computers; they ate also used as the entry/print devices in older airline and hotel reservation sys-

---

™ Registered Trademark of IBM, Inc.

tems, and as remote terminals communicating with a time-sharing host computer.

The Selectric has been in the word-processing environment as part of the IBM stand-alone magnetic tape or magnetic card typing stations. Rebuilt machines withdrawn from large systems are now available quite inexpensively, and they are enjoying a new lease on life as the hard-copy devices for personal computing systems whose owners want high-quality print but have limited budgets.

In the Selectric machine, the characters are arranged in four rows around the surface of a sphere (see Figure 6.2). Positioning with three degrees of freedom brings a character into the printing position:

- The axis may be left at its home angle to print the bottom row of characters or tilted to three other angles to bring the upper three rows into the printing position.
- The sphere may be rotated into any one of five positions right or left of the home position.
- A 180-degree rotation is equivalent to a shift.

The character code selects one, both, or neither of two tilt solenoids T1 and T2.

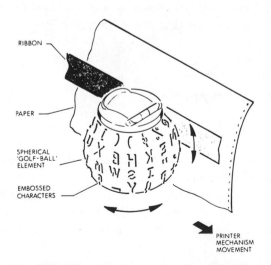

RIBBON

PAPER

SPHERICAL 'GOLF-BALL' ELEMENT

EMBOSSED CHARACTERS

PRINTER MECHANISM MOVEMENT

Figure 6.2. IBM Selectric print mechanism; simplified diagram.

There are four rotational solenoids, designated R1, R2, R2A and R5. Each is selected by one of the four least significant bits of the character code. All the unshifted characters are on the front surface of the sphere (nearest the paper); when the shift key is pressed, the sphere is rotated 180 degrees horizontally. The shifted characters are then selected by the same combinations of tilt and rotation left or right as the corresponding unshifted characters.

When the desired character is in position, a clutch connects the shaft on which the sphere is mounted to the main drive shaft, and it receives a sharp impact which moves the sphere forward to strike the character through the ribbon onto the paper.

The I/O Selectric has two advantages in a word-processing environments:

- It produces clean, good-looking print, especially if a thin-film ribbon rather than a fabric ribbon is used (the thickness and threads of the fabric result in broader lines).
- Many different typefaces are available for it; and changing the sphere takes only 5 seconds or less.

Although an office Selectric can go for many months without needing any attention except cleaning, such is not the case for the I/O Selectric. The machine has over 600 moving parts and many critical adjustments; when it is printing at the full rate of 14.9 characters per second for 5 or 6 hours a day, vibration is heavy; and even if it does not actually fail, print quality becomes unacceptable for word-processing within a few weeks and a service call is required. In a programming environment, with heavy and unskilled hands on the keyboard and very little protection from such abuse as allowing paper to ball round the platen or not cleaning dust and paper shreds out of the machine, the failure rate is even higher.

From the viewpoint of microcomputer systems, there is another disadvantage. Nearly all microcomputer hardware is ASCII-code-oriented; an 8-bit code is transmitted, least significant bit first, at one of several rates that can all be derived from a single clock generator. The I/O Selectric requires a clock which is not a multiple of available frequencies to generate a bit rate of 134.5 bits per second; it uses a 6-bit code and sends the most significant bit first. In addition, two special character codes are required for upshifting and downshifting. For this reason, interfacing an I/O Selectric to a microcomputer requires translation tables, modifications to the hardware and a much more elaborate software driver.

One other feature of the I/O Selectric requires attention. Modern microcomputer systems usually communicate with their terminals or with other computers in a full-duplex mode. That is, the keyboard is mechanically and electrically independent of the display. What is typed on the keyboard does not automatically appear on the display; the characters must either be locally routed into the display or sent to the host computer which then echoes them back. Transmission can thus take place in both directions at the same time. This makes it easy for an operator if need be to interrupt messages coming from the computer.

The I/O Selectric, on the other hand, is basically a half-duplex machine. Characters for keys pressed on the keyboard print automatically. The electronics have a "send" mode (keyboard to computer) and a "receive" mode (computer to printer). When the operator presses the return key, the return code sent to the computer is automatically followed by an EOT (end of text) code to tell the computer that a line has been completed. The electronics automatically switch to the receive mode, mechanically locking the keyboard in the process. The computer can now process the line transmitted, whether it is a text line or an operating system command. The keyboard does not unlock until the computer returns an EOA (end of address) code that switches the terminal electronics back to the send mode and unlocks the keyboard. This protocol must also be incorporated into the software driver for any Selectric terminal that simulates an IBM 2741 terminal. It is another complication for the microcomputer systems designer to take into account.

Office Selectrics can be used as printers with the aid of an electro-mechanical interface. The device consists of a set of solenoids corresponding to those of the I/O Selectric. The frame on which these are mounted fits underneath the Selectric; and the solenoid armatures are mechanically connected by rods to the appropriate character selection and function actuators of the typewriter. The adapter contains a serial communications interface, a multiple-character buffer and translation circuits to convert ASCII character codes into solenoid activation signals. This device has two advantages:

- Attachment of the device does not invalidate IBM service contracts on the typewriter.
- No special computer hardware or software are needed.

6.4 DAISY-WHEEL AND THIMBLE PRINTERS

The daisy-wheel printer is so-called because its type element resembles a daisy with "petals" radiating from the central boss (See Figure 6.3). Daisy-wheel printers are made by Diablo and Qume; and thimble printers are made by NEC (Nippon Electric Co.). A plastic daisy wheel for the standard ASCII character set has 96 of these petals, with one character embossed at the end of each. The Diablo can also accommodate metal print wheels having 88, 92 or 96 petals, according to the character set. Thirty or so typefaces are available, some suitable for proportional spacing. That is, carriage motion is not the same for all characters; letter width differs from one letter to the next. Metal print wheels are more durable than are plastic ones; they allow finer detail in the typeface and they end to give a sharper impression but slow down the print speed. The NEC Spinwriter has a print element with a horizontal boss and petals bent upward; it looks more like a thimble, and so bears that name.

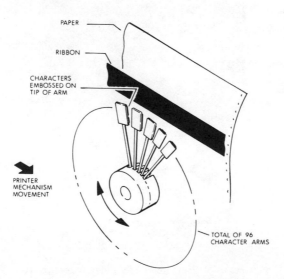

Figure 6.3. Daisy-wheel print mechanism; simplified diagram.

The print wheel is mounted on the shaft of a servo motor as shown in Figure 6.4. At power-up the wheel is brought to a home position, which depending on the wheel in use, may or may not bring a character into the print position. Each time a character code is sent to the printer, the wheel position for the character to be printed is compared with the current position of the wheel. The difference, positive or negative, represents the number of steps to be made by the motor to bring the new character into the print position. The sign of the difference and its magnitude cause the wheel to turn clockwise or counterclockwise to go through the least amount of rotation. The wheel is returned to the home position by any nonprinting ASCII code (space, carriage-return, line feed, form feed, tab and control codes).

As the wheel rotates, the ribbon is lifted into position and the carriage moves one character position (for standard type) or the width of the new character (for proportional spacing). A solenoid-driven hammer then strikes the petal (or thimble) against the ribbon to print

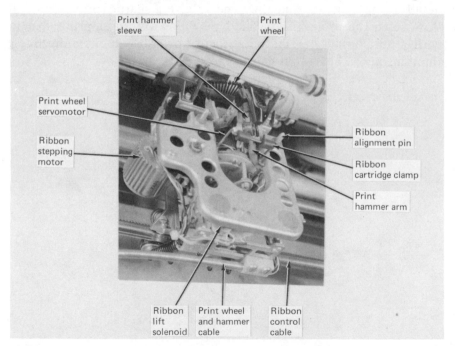

Figure 6.4. Print head of a daisy-wheel printer.

the character. The hammer force is reduced by the circuitry for certain character codes; this ensures that letters and numerals are struck with sufficient force to make a good impression, while periods, commas and other small characters are struck with less force so that they do not puncture the paper.

Platen and Carriage Mechanisms

Teletypes and Selectrics drive the platen through a pawl and ratchet and advance the paper by line increments 1/6 inch) in the upward direction only, as shown in Figure 6.5. Daisy-wheel printers drive the platen through gears by a powerful stepping motor, as shown in Figure 6.6. The increment of motion is 1/48 inch and may be applied in either direction. Software, either in the printer unit or in the host computer, controls the number of increments and the direction of movement. For alphanumeric work, a displacement of 6 increments per line gives 8 lines per inch (for elite type), and 9 increments per line gives 6 lines per inch (for pica type). In a graphics mode, any number of increments can be used. The capability for bidirectional platen movement allows the printer to produce sub- and superscripts while writing a single line—and with little loss of speed.

For horizontal carriage motion, Teletypes and Selectrics have an escapement mechanism that uses a toothed rack, as shown in Figure 6.7. As each character is printed, a double-toothed pawl allows a spring to pull the carriage one character width to the right; a carriage

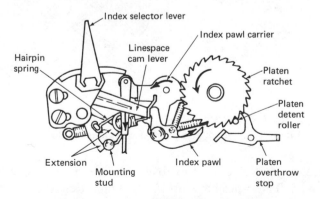

Figure 6.5. Pawl/ratchet platen drive.

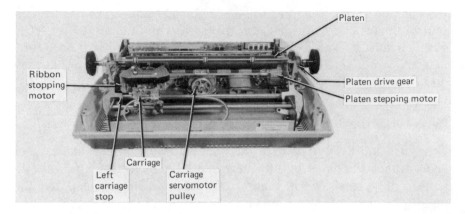

Figure 6.6.   Main components of a daisy-wheel printer.

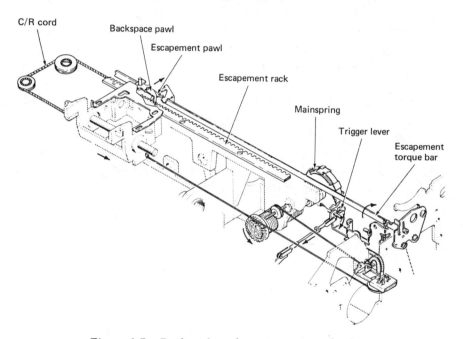

Figure 6.7.   Rack and pawl escapement mechanism.

return disengages the pawl and drives the carriage to the left under motor power. Teletypes have no tabbing facilities, and Selectrics have mechanical tab stops.

In daisy-wheel printers, the carriage may be driven in either direction by a servomotor, as shown in Figure 6.8. At power-up, the logic drives the carriage leftward until it hits the mechanical stop and then brings it to a home position approximately 1/5 inch to the right of the left stop. Thereafter, all carriage motion is controlled by comparing two counters: one contains the current displacement of the desired new carriage position. The smallest increment of motion is 1/60 inch in early models and 1/120 inch in current models. Analog arithmetic logic circuitry within the printer determines the difference between the actual and the desired position and controls the direction and velocity of the motion. Five different velocities are possible: the lower velocities are invoked at the start and when the carriage is close to the desired position (e.g., in moving to an adjacent character position); the highest velocity is invoked only during a long movement (two or more inches).

Character printing speed is limited by the time:

- To move the proper character into the print position (9 to 50 milliseconds).
- To move the carriage to the next print position (about 25 milliseconds).

Carriage returns require from 50 to 400 milliseconds; and line feeds require approximately 80 milliseconds per line. On a densely printed

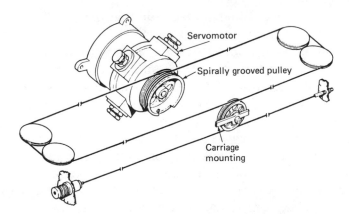

Figure 6.8.   Daisy-wheel carriage movement.

page where almost every column contains a character, the actual print speed remains close to the nominal maximum (30 to 60 characters per second). Some improvement can be obtained on sparsely printed pages if the software driver does not convert multiple spaces and/or line feeds to a motion increment until it receives the next printable character. This produces fast slewing over white space instead of stopping the carriage at each character position. Furthermore, for an indented paragraph, a carriage return should not take the carriage back to the left margin; it should stop at the indentation where printing begins. A page with much white space is thus printed faster than one with lots of text.

A further refinement made possible by the provision of two buffers in the printer is bidirectional printing. Printing starts from buffer A, from left to right. Buffer B is loaded by the computer while this line is printing. Then buffer B is inspected to compute the position of its end of line. When the carriage return at the end of line A is reached while printing, the carriage slews forward or backward to the end (right) of line B. It is now a simple matter to scan buffer B and print this line backward (from right to left). For a typical text, bidirectional printing eliminates half the carriage movement to produce a further increase in throughput. A Greek scholar of our acquaintance, when shown this in operation, remarked dryly that he was glad to see modern technology catching up to the accomplishments of his ancestors 3000 years ago, who also wrote in this "boustrophedon" fashion (i.e., like a man ploughing a field).

We should perhaps add that they
!rennam siht ni daer osla

To obtain all these new features, the universal game of engineering tradeoffs is played once again. Mechanically, the daisy-wheel printer is extremely simple: it has fewer than 12 moving parts; the Selectric has more than 600. On the other hand, the daisy-wheel printer is electrically extremely complex. The earliest model (the Diablᴐ Hytype I) contains logic boards with more than 250 TTL chips and an analog board with more than 20 chips and dozens of transistors and discrete components. In later models the chip count has been reduced by the use of large-scale integration chips, each of which provides many functions. Trading mechanical complexity for electrical complexity is a good bargain—it's the moving parts that usually cause problems. Modern logic chips and transistors seldom fail. For example, a group of eight terminals equipped with daisy-wheel printers had only one service call in 6 months—and the problem was in the keyboard. The printers have been in use 6 hours per day for nearly 2 years without a single printer failure. The only maintenance necessary has been regular cleaning and the replacement of print wheels and ribbons.

7
Medium-Speed Printers

Higher printing speed (120 or more characters per second) requires a different approach. For many years, the only possibilities were the drum or chain printers used with large computers; size and cost (purchase or lease and maintenance) made them unsuitable for microcomcomputer systems. During the last decade, however, new technologies have developed. As a result, small, reliable and fast printers have appeared on the market at moderate prices.

The three mechanisms of medium-speed printers are:

- Band and belt-type arrays.
- Impact dot matrix.
- Ink-jet dot matrix.

7.1 BAND AND BELT PRINTERS

Band and belt printers operate on the same basic principle, shown in Figure 7.1. Multiple sets of the character alphabet are carried past groups of print hammers. The characters are etched or embossed:

- On the scalloped edge of a band.
- On metallic slugs embedded in a polyurethane belt (Figure 7.1).

The belt is driven by pulleys (which are outside the print area) of such diameter as to put minimum strain on the belt at the designed

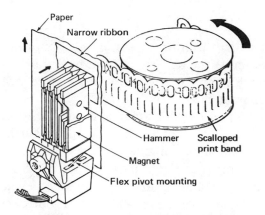

Figure 7.1. Band/belt printer mechanism.

rotation speed. Higher rotational speed contributes to higher print speed. Rotational speed is limited by the durability of the material of which the belt is made. Polyurethane belts yield print speeds between 30 and 200 characters per second. Steel bands yield speeds up to 3000 lines per minute, or 50 lines per second of 80 to 132 characters each. That is 4,000 to 6,400 characters per minute for expensive printers. Medium-priced printers produce 400 to 800 characters per minute.

One solenoid-actuated hammer for each of the 80 or 132 print positions is energized when the character to be printed in that column arrives under it. The belt may carry several character sets. Several print characters often arrive simultaneously under the correct hammers, so that the line is printed in a fraction of a complete rotation of the belt.

The printer has one or more print buffers, each holding a complete line. With two buffers, one buffer is used for printing while the other is refilled. A character set buffer, with one position for each hammer, is loaded with characters in the order in which they occur on the belt. Timing pulses, generated by the drive train, reload this buffer as the belt moves, so that as a type slug arrives over a hammer, the character code is found in the corresponding position of the character set buffer. When the print buffer and the character set buffer contain the same character in corresponding positions, the associated hammer solenoid is energized and the character prints.

7.2 IMPACT DOT MATRIX PRINTERS

An impact dot matrix printer (or simply *matrix printer* has a print head that moves across the paper; the print head consists of solenoids striking thin flexible rods arranged in one or more vertical columns (Figure 7.2). Characters are built on a 5 × 7 (or 7 × 9) dot matrix in a way similar to that by which characters are built on a CRT tube. However, the head sweeps out the full character height. Horizontal movement is in increments of one matrix column; all the strikers needed for that column of the matrix are activated simultaneously.

To print an E, for example, all seven (or nine) solenoids are fired at the same time to produce the left-hand vertical stroke; the top, center and bottom solenoids are fired together on succeeding horizontal steps to make the horizontal strokes.

The codes of all characters to be printed in the line are in the print buffer in the desired order. As the head advances across the paper, one dot width at a time, the ASCII code for the character to be printed and the matrix column number are combined to address the character generator. This is arranged differently from that for the CRT—by column instead of by row. The output of the character generator is a binary sequence conveying a vertical dot pattern with 1s representing the strikers activated (Figure 7.3). Thus, for a 9 × 7 matrix, the same ASCII code appears seven times in the character generator address, but in combination with matrix column numbers from 1 to 7.

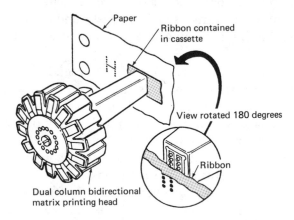

Figure 7.2. Impact dot matrix printer mechanism.

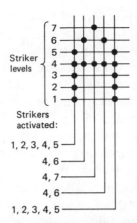

Figure 7.3.   Character building with a dot matrix printer.

At each access the strikers corresponding to 1s are activated. After the seventh access, the current character has been completely printed; the print head then moves one more column for the intercharacter space, when no strikers are activated.

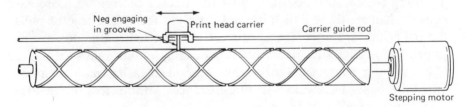

Figure 7.4.   Carriage drive of dot matrix printer.

The hardware of a dot matrix printer is relatively simple. The print head is attached to a carriage mounted on low-friction rollers for easy horizontal movement (Figure 7.4). The carriage maintains accurate alignment and spacing between the print head and the platen. A peg at the center of the carriage projects downward to engage in a spiral trough cut in a roller that rotates below the guide rails (Figure 7.4). This roller is driven by a stepping motor. The pitch of the spiral allows high-speed carriage movement. However, tolerances are kept tight to ensure precise carriage positioning.

The most delicate part of the mechanism is the print head, which consists of the solenoids and the flexible strikers that slide in curved channels. The flat printing face of a striker is often no greater than 1/100 inch in diameter.

The paper is moved vertically up or down by another stepping motor. The space between two strikers is usually the stepping increment. On small printers, the paper is held against the platen by rubber rollers; the pressure is sufficient to ensure that rotating the platen moves the paper without slippage. This friction feed has advantages for graphics work, where it may be necessary to move the paper sometimes upward and sometimes downward over a single page as the print head traverses the printing area. When many pages are to be printed successively, friction feed may allow lateral slippage of the paper unless the pressure of the rubber rollers is completely even.

A rugged printer, used only for alphabetic printing in large quantities, may have a pin-feed platen (Figure 7.5). Here, pins at the outer edges of the platen engage performation in the paper. Alternatively, there may be provision for a removable forms tractor (Figure 7.6) that is driven by the platen motor. The forms tractor requires a larger platen motor than friction feed and consequently a larger power supply also. Hence, printers that allow the tractor option are more expensive than are those which use only friction feed. The tractor pulls the paper upward only; it can move the paper half a line downward to print subscripts and superscripts, for example; but unless the paper is kept under backward tension by some means, the tractor cannot move the paper backward for long distances without loss of registration due to buckling of the paper.

Most dot matrix printers are equipped with a microprocessor controller to handle all the logic of print head movement, paper movement, striker actuation and interfacing with the host computer. The controller program is in read-only memory; in addition, there is sufficient read/write memory to provide work space for the program and one or more buffers that each hold one complete row of characters.

Bidirectional Printing

Many dot matrix printers print in both directions. The current line and the next line are held in buffers. The print head position at completion of the current line is precisely known. The controller program computes the distance and direction to the end of the next line and moves the print head directly there without returning it to the left

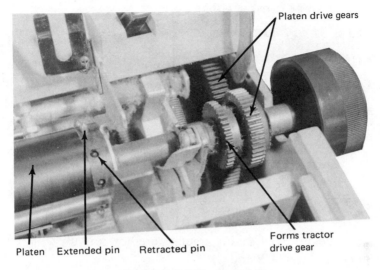

Platen drive gears

Forms tractor
drive gear

Platen   Extended pin   Retracted pin

Figure 7.5. Pin-feed platen.

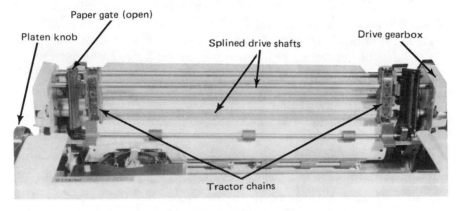

Paper gate (open)

Platen knob

Splined drive shafts

Drive gearbox

Tractor chains

Figure 7.6. Forms tractor.

margin. The number of lines per minute printed is hence substantially increased.

Multiple Print Sizes

Some dot matrix printers can print several sizes of character in the same font either by altering the height-to-width ratio for all characters of the set or by printing each column twice instead of once. Charac-

A. THIS IS A SAMPLE OF STANDARD PRINT.

B. THIS IS DOUBLE WIDTH PRINT.

C. THIS IS A SAMPLE OF VERY COMPRESSED PRINT.

D. THIS LINE IS EMPHASIZED.

E. THIS IS A LINE OF DOUBLE-STRIKE.

F. THIS IS A LINE OF DOUBLE-STRIKE EMPHASIZED.

This is the lower case with descenders, q,y,p,g,j.

Figure 7.7. Compression/expansion of dot matrix characters.

ter height is usually fixed, and characters are horizontally compressed
or expanded (Figure 7.7B and C).

Compression is obtained by reducing the horizontal displacement
between matrix columns. Expansion is obtained by generating characters with double-thickness vertical strokes and more space between
matrix columns. Selection of compressed, normal or expanded characters may be controlled either by turning on a switch or by sending
the printer a sequence of control (nonprintable) characters. This
causes the controller to access a different print routing and different
constants from the read-only memory.

Multiple-Pass Printing

One disadvantage common to all the inexpensive dot matrix printers
is that each individual dot is distinguishable. For this reason, matrix
printers cannot produce the print quality of formed-character printers
(those which print from a character embossed on a wheel or slug).
More sophisticated dot matrix printers, in the $2,000 to $5,000 price
range, overcome this disadvantage by making two, three or even four
passes over the same row of characters. Consider that each printed
dot is less than 1/100 inch in diameter. The first pass produces the
letter's outline. For the second pass, the paper is moved up a little.
The new dot pattern fills in the letter, as do successive passes. Horizontal fill-in may also be used to get more dots per inch. Gaps between dots are hence filled in, curves are smoothed and clean, sharp

letters result (Figure 7.7D). It is as though a 20 X 28 array (say) were used instead of a 5 X 7. Some printers provide program-selectable character generators for several different fonts; or one font can include italic and bold. Pluggable ROMs make it easy to change fonts. Also, the same font may be used in single- or multiple-pass mode; the former is great for drafts, producing them very rapidly; the latter unhurriedly produces final quality work (Figure 7.8). Where multiple-pass capability is present, it is usually selectable under program control.

```
!"#$%&'()*+,-./0123456789:; =¢?
@ABCDEFGHIJKLMNOPQRSTUVWXYZ[\]▵¢
\abcdefghijklmnopqrstuvwxyz |

!"#$%&'()*+,-./0123456789:; =¢?
@ABCDEFGHIJKLMNOPQRSTUVWXYZ[\]▵¢
\abcdefghijklmnopqrstuvwxyz |
```

Figure 7.8. Multipass printing.

7.3 INK JET PRINTERS

Continuous Jet Printers

Ink jet printers also construct characters from separate dots but do not have any strikers or ribbon. Instead, the print head projects tiny droplets of ink onto the paper. A system to do this is shown in Figure 7.9. Ink from a reservoir is pumped at low pressure into a projector consisting of a small cavity with a nozzle in the front wall. The back wall consists of a piezoelectric crystal to propel the ink. The droplet passes between deflector plates which let the jet hit the paper to make a dot, or deflect the ink into a gutter to be recycled and hence produce no dot.

When a voltage is applied across two opposite faces of a quartz or Rochelle salt crystal, the entire crystal physically deforms. The direction of the deformation depends upon the polarity of the applied voltage and the crystal alignment; the amount of movement is proportional to the amplitude of the voltage, within limits. When the voltage is removed, the crystal returns to its original shape. This property of crystals has been known for many decades, and has been widely

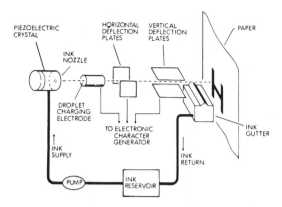

Figure 7.9.   Continuous ink jet printer.

used to control precisely the frequency of electronic oscillators used in radio transmitters. Since World War II, piezoelectric crystals have also been used as generators of ultrasonic waves in the frequency range of 25,000 to 80,000 hertz for sonar applications. At sea, these include depth sounders, fish finders and sophisticated underwater tracking equipment; on land they include burglar alarms.

In the projector of an ink jet printer, applying a short, high voltage pulse to the crystal ejects a droplet of ink through the nozzle at relatively high velocity. The droplet passes through a cylindrical electrode and acquires an electrical charge. Two pairs of deflection plates, connected to voltage amplifiers driven by the character generator, deflect the charged ink droplet up, down, left or right within the rectangular area on which the character is centered.

Pulses are applied continuously to the piezoelectric projector to obtain a steady stream of droplets. As the assembly passes over areas to the left blank, the vertical deflection plates deflect the droplets downward into a gutter by which they are returned to the reservoir. When a character is to be printed, the deflection voltages scan the character area, column by column, starting at the left. The crystal is producing a continuous sequence of pulses, which would produce vertical lines. But some dots are not printed because the droplet is deflected into the gutter. A character generator ROM is consulted for each vertical column of each character; the set of 0s and 1s obtained determines whether the droplet hits the paper or is deflected away.

When that column has been completed, the horizontal deflection voltage moves the jet one column to the right, and a new vertical scan starts.

When the entire character area has been scanned, the jet is deflected downward to the gutter while the carriage moves rightward by one character width plus the intercharacter space. Then scanning of the next character position begins.

Ink-on-Demand Printers

Another type of ink jet printer is shown in Figure 7.10. The action here is more like that of an impact dot matrix printer. The print head has one independently controlled droplet projector for each vertical element of the matrix. Ink is supplied from a pressurized cartridge through a filter and pressure-regulating system that ensures constant droplet size. The projectors for all the dots to be printed in one vertical column of the matrix are activated simultaneously by applying a pulse to the crystal. No pulse is applied to projectors for undots. The carriage then moves rightward the width of one matrix column instead of a whole character width, as in the continuous-stream printers.

Timing is critical in both types of ink jet printer; the print head manufacturing technology is still new. Hence, ink jet printers have hitherto been restricted to the upper-price brackets. However, at least one manufacturer is producing an ink jet printer for less than

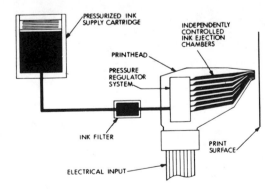

Figure 7.10. On-demand ink jet printer.

$1,000. As the technology improves, ink jet printers may take away some of the market for impact dot matrix printers. The ink jet machines are faster and quieter and have long print head life. In addition, the print quality is sometimes much better; and since droplet size remains constant throughout the life of the ink cartridge, the print quality does not degrade over ribbon life (there is no ribbon) as is the case with an impact machine.

8
Peripherals for Graphics

Peripherals for graphics fall into the following general categories:

Video
- Refresh raster displays.
- Stroke-written refresh displays.
- Stroke-written storage-tube displays.

Hard copy
- Printers.
- *X-Y* Plotters.

Input
- Standard keyboards.
- *X-Y* Coordinate digitizers.
- Light Pens.

The type of input device recommended depends upon the application and the resolution required.

8.1 VIDEO DEVICES

Refresh Raster Displays

The simplest form of refresh raster display is a standard video display provided with a special character generator. The ASCII character set contains only 128 displayable characters (including special pictorials to represent nonprinting control characters). Any character may be selected for display by the 7-bit code which represents it. An eighth bit may have various purposes: in transmission between the computer and a terminal, it provides parity; however, even if the parity bit is checked, it is stripped off again by the device. Within a terminal or video display board, the eighth bit is often used to select an emphasis tool, such as reversed video or half-brightness.

In a terminal or display board designed for low-resolution graphics, the eighth bit can select a graphics alphabet of 128 symbols from a 256-byte character generator ROM containing these as well as the alphanumerics. This technique appears in a number of personal computers (such as the Apple and Pet) and video display boards. Character and graphics generators generally provide a set of basic graphic forms from which visual displays can be built. Some of the forms can be reprogrammed and altered by the user to provide personalized designs to his specifications.

A form generator builds pixels, that is, picture elements, on the same dot-matrix as characters. Since a pixel is character size, the screen displays only as many pixels as characters. The 24 × 80 display in graphics mode presents 1,920 pixels. Nevertheless, with a well-designed "graphics alphabet" and clever programming, interesting designs can be produced even at this low resolution, especially on a color display.

Resolution is improved if the display hardware has a graphics mode in which the pixels are smaller, so that more of them can be printed on the screen. Some display drivers view the screen as a matrix of 220 × 180 elements. Refresh memory defines the color and intensity of each element. With this technique it is possible to draw curves and diagonals that seem fairly smooth and continuous—which is not the case with character-sized pixels.

Stroke-Written Refresh Displays

Stroke-written refresh displays provide much higher resolution, since they divide the screen into 1-dot pixels instead of rectangular N-dot pixels. This allows thin lines to be drawn. Curves are constructed from a series of short straight lines. The line drawn can be focused to approximately 0.015 inch in width. The screen is dot-addressable,

that is, a particular dot can be named. Typical resolution is 1,024 ×
2,048 points. A line is specified by naming its terminal coordinates.
Two digital-to-analog converters in the display hardware control the
X and *Y* deflection potentials.

To draw a line, the hardware is first furnished with the digital coordinates of the starting point. These are converted into two analog
voltages and are sent to the horizontal and vertical deflection plates to
position the beam at the right place. The coordinates of the end
point are then found and converted into voltage equivalents.

A sweep generator is then activated. It produces a uniform-change
horizontal deflection voltage to move the beam from X1 to X2 linearly. The sweeps are set to start and end at the same time; the beam is
turned on at the start and off at the end; hence, a line is drawn on
the screen. All this happens very fast, so that the next line may be
drawn from the ending point of the first without turning off the beam.
If desired, the beam may be turned off and moved to a new starting
location elsewhere on the screen. The action is analogous to that of
an *X-Y* plotter, in which the carriage is moved to a start location, a
"pen-down" command is given and the carriage is then moved linearly
to the ending coordinates.

Unlike raster displays, in which drawing always takes place left to
right and top to bottom of the screen, stroke-written displays can draw
lines anywhere on the screen in any order. Memory locations are accessed sequentially by a counter which conveys the order in which
lines are drawn. The content of a memory location contains an *X* or
Y coordinate value defining beam position.

This CR display, like any other with short-persistence screen, must
be refreshed at least 30 times per second to avoid flicker. Thus, the
number of lines that can be drawn depends on the writing speed of
the CRT and the buffer size provided, when the display is directly
connected to the host computer. For a remote display connected to
the host by a telephone line, picture complexity is limited by the rate
at which coordinates can be transmitted.

Stroke-written refresh display generators work best when large
amounts of memory are available to them, with high transfer speeds.
But display updating can take place very quickly—as quickly, in fact,
as the host computer can compute the modifications. Displays of
this type are therefore well suited to applications where new view-

points are needed in quick succession, or where the user wishes to see the effect of a modification immediately. Thus, he may see a cube rotating on the display and get a view from all angles. He can stop it, alter it and then rotate it again.

Stroke-Written Storage-Tube Displays

Storage tubes have a phosphor with long persistence. Once a line has been drawn on this CRT, it remains visible for several hours without any refreshing. However, individual lines cannot be erased as they can be on stroke-written refresh displays. The entire screen has to be erased by flooding it with a cloud of electrons from a special erasing source that is contained within the tube but is separate from the electron gun used for drawing. Vectors are drawn in the same way as in stroke-written refresh displays. However, because no refreshing is needed and writing speeds are slower, memory requirements and transfer speeds are lower. As an example, if 2,000 vectors are required in a design, a relatively small amount of memory can be used as a double buffer; the host computer computes N vectors and stores the coordinates in buffer A; when then buffer is full, control of it is passed to the communications driver, while the graphics driver starts filling buffer B.

Long-persistence displays are well suited to remote-display terminals driven from a host over low-speed telephone lines, and for applications in which many short vectors are generated but where immediate update and modification is not a requirement. Typical is the Tektronix 4011, a complete microprocessor-driven graphics device. It can generate displays using the internal BASIC interpreter which has special plotting statements. It can also be driven from a host computer with greater storage and computing capabilities over a telephone line, and has a built-in acoustic coupler for this purpose.

8.2 HARD COPY

Printers

Formed-character printers, such as the daisy wheel or Spinwriter types, are ideally suited for producing graphs and histograms. Bidirectional carriage and platen movement in horizontal increments of 1/120 inch and vertical increments of 1/48 inch allow several curves to be plotted on the same axes and distinguished from each other by different plotting characters. Lines are drawn by sending a character sequence specifying an X distance and a Y distance from the current print head position and the character to be printed on completion of the vector. Several terminals and printers are capable of responding to standard Calcomp plotter software routines; an example generated in this way is shown in Figure 8.1.

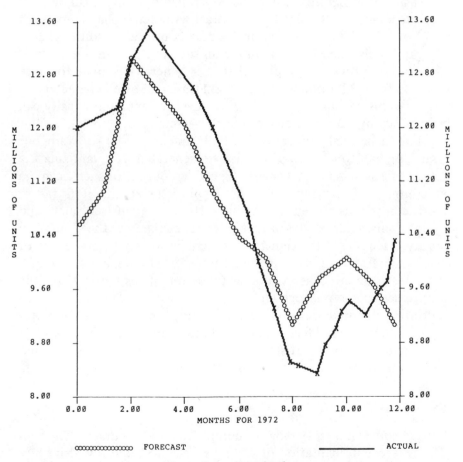

Figure 8.1. Sample plot.

Formed-character printers can also produce pictorial output. They restrict the user to character-sized pixels, but it is possible to produce designs with higher resolution than that for CRT. The printer is not limited to an explicit number of pixels, as with the CRT display. A common printer width is 132 characters, but there is little restriction on the number of rows used. If, for example, the picture is built on two sheets of 14 X 11 inch paper, the printout has 120 X 132 = 15,840 pixels; each individual pixel is thus a much smaller percentage of the total picture than in the 80 X 24 = 1,920 pixels available on the CRT screen.

Density of a picture area can be controlled by using small or open characters (such as ".". or '0') to contrast with dense characters (such as '??' or '*'). On daisy-wheel or dot matrix printers, additional density can be obtained by overstriking on the same line. Some dot matrix printers provide a graphic character generator similar to those available for CRT displays. Printers that use embossed characters do not have this capability, but 10 or 12 levels of apparent density can be obtained by careful choice of the characters used.

Printer-generated pictures can be built up entirely by software, but a kind of half-tone picture can also be generated by quantizing the output of a slow-scan TV camera. The video output of such a camera has continuously varying density levels on each scan line of the raster; if this continuous range is divided into 10 or 12 quantized values and a printer character is chosen that gives approximately the same pixel density, each line of the camera raster can be translated into a row of characters. For a 22 X 14 inch picture, viewed from a distance of 8 to 10 feet, the effect is as good as (and sometimes better than) the average newspaper photograph.

Printer-generated pictorial material is not limited to the computer portraits that stall holders at fairs produce by digitizing the output of a TV camera. Serious artists produce fabric designs, abstract art and studies for works to be executed in other media.

X-Y Plotters

Plotters come in a wide range of complexity and accuracy. The simplest is a recent adaptation of a child's Etch-a-Sketch toy, driven by stepping motors from a microprocessor. This has very limited resolution and very poor curve and diagonal drawing ability. The most complex and expensive, such as the Calcomp or Hewlett-Packard, have a resolution of 1/1000 inch, a drawing area of several feet in each direction and multiple pens. These are used in scientific and engineering environments and for cartography, among other applications.

A plotter in the $750 to $1,500 price range has a single pen mounted on a carriage driven in both X and Y directions by stepping motors, in increments of about 1/200 inch, and a drawing area of about 8-1/2 X 11 inches. Like the stroke-written CRT displays, this draws straight lines with starting and ending X-Y coordinates specified as 16-bit numbers. Pen-up and pen-down commands are standard, so that the various parts of the drawing can be executed in the most convenient order and do not have to be continuous. Software for this plotter usually provides a pause with a console message, so that a pen with a new color of ink can be inserted in the carriage.

8.3 INPUT DEVICES

Standard Keyboards

Standard console keyboards can be used as crude input devices for building and modifying simple graphic displays if provided with a repeat function either by a key hold-down or a separate key. This either moves the cursor quickly around the screen or generates a block of identical characters. Alternatively, the program can interpret the character received to modify the display according to more complex rules. Keyboards are not ideal as graphic input devices.

X-Y Coordinate Digitizers

X-Y coordinate digitizers are of two general types:

- Devices that initially generate an analog signal that is converted to digital form.
- Devices that generate discrete digital pulses which clock a counter up or down.

Analog Devices

A paddle or joystick supplied with TV games is an analog device. The paddle consists of a rod, pivoted at or near its center on a universal ball joint that allows two simultaneous degrees of movement: forward/back and left/right. The upper part of the rod above the ball joint is the handle; the lower part engages in two semicircular, slotted metal strips attached at their extremities to potentiometer spindles. The strips cross each other at right angles, and the control rod pokes through the small rectangle formed at their meeting point.

If the control rod is pushed forward or back, it slides freely through the slot of the north-south strip without moving it: but it displaces the east-west strip and thereby rotates the corresponding potentiometers. Similarly, moving the paddle left to right causes the north-south strip to be displaced. Moving the paddle diagonally causes both sets of potentiometers to be rotated.

Conversion.   A constant reference voltage is applied between the top of one potentiometer in each plane and ground. Linear potentiometers are used so that the voltage appearing on the slider is proportional to paddle displacement in that plane. Each voltage (X and Y) is applied to a voltage-to-frequency (V-F) converter chip. Movement of the paddle from full back (or left) to full forward (or right) varies the output frequency of this V-F chip from (typically) 10 to 10,000 hertz. The chip output is a square wave that is applied to a counter sampled by a clock; the forward/back and left/right counts are hence proportional to the paddle position and define for the display program the column (X) and row (Y) position of the cursor on the screen, which may then be moved to be displayed to the operator.

Digital Devices

A digital device converts rotational or linear mechanical displacement to electric signals but does so in discrete steps. The paddle described above moves a potentiometer to generate an analog signal that is then converted to a train of discrete pulses. We can generate discrete pulses directly, if we remove the potentiometer from the paddle and replace it by an opaque disk, having a series of holes and its circumference that pass between a lamp and a photocell. Each time a hole passes the lamp, the photocell generates a pulse which increments a counter.

A single row of holes in the disk detects movement of the disk but not the direction of movement. Consider a double set of holes, one having a slight angular displacement from the other and a separate photocell for each set. Then the direction, as well as the amount of movement, is indicated by the order in which the photocells generate pulses; detection logic can then route a single set of pulses to either the UP or DOWN input of an up/down counter.

The same principle applies to a drawing bed on which a drawing to be digitized is placed. A carriage capable of moving in two orthogonal directions (X and Y) carries a stylus over the paper. First, place the carriage in the top left corner of the area and generate an initializing signal to reset the X and Y counters. Thereafter, moving the carriage generates a train of up or down pulses proportional to the amount of movement, so that the position of the carriage is always known by the computer. Pressing the stylus down onto the drawing to be copied generates a "copy" signal, so that each segment of the line followed is defined as increments of X or Y from the starting point.

Light Pen

A light pen is used to indicate a point of interest on a CRT display. This may be a line that is to be changed in a drawing, or a command selected from a menu for execution.

The light pen consists of a cylindrical casing containing a lens and photocell. The photocell output is small if the light pen is over a dark area on the screen and larger if it is over a light area. This voltage is shaped into a pulse which is then combined with signals from the display circuitry. In a raster display, the light pen pulse causes the column and row counters to be sampled; the combined count represents the X and Y coordinates of the light pen on the screen. The program can then take the appropriate action.

III
STORAGE

9
Introduction to External Storage

9.1 GENERAL PRINCIPLES

We have described storage—that is, memory—that is directly address-able by the microprocessor. But in microcomputer systems there are two limitations on this kind of memory:

- Volatility.
- Addressability.

Volatility means that when power is turned off, the data stored in the memory disappears.

The number of lines in the address bus governs the addressability —that is, the amount of memory that can be addressed by the CPU. The 8-bit microprocessors usually have 16 address lines to address randomly 64K bytes. The IEEE Standard S-100 bus provides a fur-ther four address lines to select up to 16 banks of 64K each—i.e., a total of just over 1 megabyte. To switch from one bank to another, a software routine is used. This adds overhead to program execution time, but only when bank switching is done. Other 16-bit micropro-cessors have 20 address lines to address up to 1 megabyte of memory.

External storage is a necessity, both to preserve operating systems and user programs when the computer is powered down and to handle larger quantities of data than can be accommodated in memory. And computer systems are subject to a variation of Parkinson's law: "Sys-tem requirements always grow to exceed available memory."

Types of Media

A *medium* is a physical material, the surface of which can be altered in some way. *Writing* data alters the originally homogenous surface in some manner that directly corresponds to the binary data written; the *reading* of the medium detects the alterations made by writing and recovers the data. Some methods of recording permanently change the medium (for example, by punching a hole in it); these methods are termed *destructive*, and the medium is *nonreusable*. Other methods make changes to the medium that can be erased or overwritten; these methods are *nondestructive* and the medium is *reusable*. The principal methods of recording media in microcomputer systems are:

- *Mechanical.* Paper is removed from a punched card or paper tape to indicate the prescence of a 1. Destructive; medium nonreusable.
  Punched cards.
  Paper tapes.
- *Optical.* An ink or pencil mark is made at a bit site to indicate the presence of a 1. Destructive: medium nonreusable.
  Mark sensing cards.
- *Magnetic.* Magnetic patterns are superimposed on the medium; the nature of the pattern determines whether a 1 or a 0 is recorded. Nondestructive: medium reusable.
  Magnetic tapes (open reel or cassettes).
  Magnetic disks (hard disk or floppy disk).

These media can also be classified by their suitability for sequential or direct access to records stored on them.

Sequential access implies that access is possible only in the order in which records appear on the medium. If we wish to read the seventy-second record from a punch-card deck, paper tape or magnetic tape, we have to start at the beginning of the deck or tape and read records 1 through 71, counting them or reading identifiers, before we can find 72.

Direct access implies that any specified record stored on the medium can be found and read within a short time. Direct access to magnetic tape records is theoretically possible, but the average access time for a specified record would be approximately 10 seconds for a high-speed open-reel tape and 20 to 60 seconds for a cassette. This makes direct access impractical for magnetic tapes. It is impossible for punch-card decks or mark sensing equipment. On magnetic disks, however, the average access time is only a few milliseconds: and direct access is both practical and convenient, although still slower than sequential access of consecutive records.

9.2 PUNCH CARDS

The geometry of the most common form of punch card is shown in Figure 9.1. This format is variously called the 80-column card, the Hollerith card or the IBM card. Notice that there are 80 frames in one direction and 12 in the other. Each type of frame has a name; we say that there are 80 *columns* and 12 *rows*. The intersection of a column and a row creates a hole site. At this intersection a hole may or may not be punched. When present, the hole designates a 1.

The most popular way of representing information in the punch card is the *Hollerith* code, shown in Figure 9.1. A record can consist of up to 80 characters, each character of the record occupying one

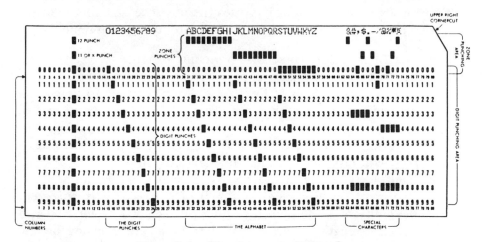

Figure 9.1. 80-column punched card.

complete column. The code for a numeric character consists of a single hole punched in the row corresponding to the numeral. An alphabetic character is represented by two holes, of which one is in one of the rows 1 through 9, and the other in one of the *zone rows* (12, 11, or 0). Special characters (punctuation and symbols) may require more than two holes.

Punched cards are seldom used in microcomputer systems, partly because both punching and reading are slower than writing and reading on other media. A more cogent reason is that card punches and readers are bulky, power-hungry and an order of magnitude more expensive than read/write equipment for other media. The cards themselves are bulky and more expensive than other media on a cost-per-byte basis. For complete systems costing less than $12,000, it is not economical to attach punch-card equipment that costs more than twice that amount and occupies three times the space required by the rest of the system.

9.3 PAPER TAPE

Physical

A paper tape about four thousandths of an inch (0.004 inch) is the medium. Information is recorded by punching holes to indicate the presence of a 1 and is read by moving the tape past a reading station that mechanically or optically senses the presence of a hole. The paper is specially manufactured to meet the following requirements.

- The fiber is selected so that punching produces a clean, round hole with no ragged edges.
- The tensile strength of the paper allows the tape to be wound on reels and spooled from one to another at speeds up to 120 inches per second without deforming the holes or breaking.
- Tape manufactured for optical readers is opaque or provides a good contrast ratio between hole and no hole.
- Fan-fold tape is creased every 8-1/2 inches to form a flat stack, instead of being wound on a reel. The creases have sufficient flexibility to lie flat when passing through the reader, and sufficient strength not to tear if data holes are punched on the crease.

The width of the tape depends upon the number of bits per transverse frame. Standard tape widths are somewhat over 1/2 inch for a 5-bit frame, and 1 inch for a frame of 7 or 8 bits.

Tape is generally supplied in 1,000-foot reels. The length of an individual paper tape file depends upon the amount of data punched, and may vary from a few inches to several hundred feet, with 6 to 8 inches of blank leader at each end. There are 10 frames (characters) per inch; maximum punching speed is 50 to 80 characters per second. Standard reading speeds are 10 characters per second for Teletype mechanical readers; 50 characters per second for some mechanical readers; 300 characters per second for optical readers; and 1,000 characters per second for high-speed optical readers. All the above are motor-driven. For microcomputer systems where reading paper tape is only an occasional necessity, there are also optical readers through which the tape is pulled by hand; these can read up to 5,000 characters per second.

Tape Geometry

A diagram of a typical 8-level paper tape is shown in Figure 9.2. The least-significant-bit position is the leftmost of the three levels to the left of the small sprocket holes; the most-significant-bit position is the rightmost of the levels to the right of the sprocket holes. There are two, three, or five of these levels for five-level, six-level, and eight-level tapes, respectively.

Note that the sprocket holes are smaller than the data holes and are displaced so that the trailing edges (not the centers) are aligned with the data holes. These sprocket holes serve two purposes:

- In mechanical readers, they engage the teeth of the drive sprocket. The sprocket rotates in steps not continuously; but when the sprocket stops, the sprocket teeth and the tape guides position the tape so that any holes are exactly over the mechanical sensing fingers.
- In 300-characters per second and 1,000-characters per second optical readers there is no sprocket; the tape is driven by a rubber-tired capstan and a pressure roller. The capstan is usually driven by a stepper motor. Light passes through the holes to photocells

which generate an electric signal; the signal generated by the sprocket hole in a particular frame is slightly delayed with respect to the data signals. Using the leading edge of this delayed signal as a "data ready" strobe ensures that reading takes place only when the data has stabilized, and minimizes any slight skew in the tape itself.

Tape Codes

Eight-level tapes permit punching bytes containing binary data directly usable by microprocessors as instruction, address or data bytes. Alternatively, 7 bits may specify an ASCII character code, while the eighth is used as a parity bit. For this reason, the readers and punches most commonly used with microcomputer systems use 1-inch tape and have eight-level capability.

Six-level readers and punches are most commonly found in terminals based on the IBM I/O Selectric typewriter. Six bits provide only 64 combinations, which is not sufficient for all the characters

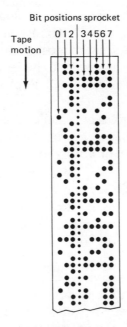

Figure 9.2. Punched paper tape.

needed. The 6-bit EBCDIC and Correspondence codes therefore include an up-shift code and a down-shift code. All characters that follow an up-shift are interpreted as uppercase until a down-shift code is encountered; thereafter, all characters are interpreted as lowercase until another upshift is encountered.

Five-level readers and punches are found only on old Teletypes (Model 28 and earlier). The 5 bits provide only 32 combinations; the code set therefore contains a letters code and a numerals code, which act in much the same way as the up-shift and down-shift codes of the six-level tapes. Because the complete character set contains only 64 codes, lowercase letters are not provided and the special character set is limited. Baudot code is the standard for five-level tapes, which are now found only in personal microcomputer systems and in communications terminals used by the deaf.

Selection and Movement

Mechanical and manual readers move the tape in the forward direction only. Thus, if a character is not properly sensed, it is not possible to return and automatically reexamine it. For this reason, data is usually punched in blocks, with a check byte at the end of every block. If the reading routine detects an error, operator intervention is required to move the tape back so that the erroneous block can be reread. The 300-character per second optical readers sometimes, though not always, have the capability of reading in either direction; with appropriate software drivers, these readers can automatically reread a block in which an error was detected.

9.4 MAGNETIC TAPE

The magnetic tape used in microcomputers is 1/4 inch wide for cartridge and open-reel drives, and 1/8 inch wide for cassette drives. Thickness depends on the amount of tape on the reel, but it is either 1-1/2 thousandths of an inch, (1,200-foot open reel or 300-foot cartridge) or 1 thousandth of an inch (450-foot cartridge or 30-minute cassette). Half-mil tape is available for audio uses, but it is unsuitable for digital recordings because it tends to stretch in use.

One side of the tape has a magnetic coating of ferric oxide (Fe_2O_3) or chromium dioxide (CrO_2) and passes over the recording and playback heads, in intimate contact with them. The coated side of the tape has little sheen; whereas the uncoated side shows a high gloss. At each end of the tape there may be a "leader" of uncoated mylar, in length equivalent to about two turns of a full reel (or cartridge hub). This leader serves the dual purpose of protecting the ends of the recordable area and allowing photoelectric sensing of the beginning and end of the tape.

10
Magnetic Recording Methods

Methods of recording a digital data stream on magnetic media and in recovering the data upon playback fall into two classes:

- Analog.
- Saturation.

This choice affects not only the read/write electronics but also the design of the recording and playback heads and, to some extent, the magnetic characteristics of the tape to be used. The two methods are incompatible. Audio tape drives cannot be used for saturation recording, nor can digital tape drives be used for analog recording of audio signals.

Within each group there is a further choice of encoding methods—that is, the manner in which 1s and 0s are represented. The encoding method governs the maximum density of the recorded data and, therefore, the maximum transfer rate.

Cassette recorders and floppy disk drives are *bit serial* devices, recording only one track at a time. In large computers, the recording methods we discuss are applied to seven- or nine-track tape drives, or to hard disks with multiple heads, which are *bit parallel, word serial* devices. Microcomputers do not use these devices, so our discussions and illustrations assume single-track drives.

10.1 ANALOG RECORDING

Analog recording is typically encountered in a microcomputer system with a standard audio tape or cassette drive. This keeps system cost low. The heads and electronics of audio recorders are designed to handle signals of varying amplitude within the range of 20 to 20,000 hertz. The magnetic characteristics of audio tapes are optimized for the recording and reproduction of such signals.

There are several possible ways of encoding a digital bit stream into audio:

- Single-tone on/off keying.
- Single- or dual-tone pulse ratio encoding.
- Dual-tone frequency-shift keying.
- Dual-tone phase encoding.

Single-Tone On/Off Keying

Records a tone burst lasting one bit time for each bit cell containing a logic 1 and no tone for a logic 0, as shown in Figure 10.1A. This method is satisfactory for slow transfer rates up to 10 characters per second, but it is highly speed-sensitive, because accurate playback depends on a bit clock generated on the interface board; thus tape-speed variations exceeding 2 or 3 percent may make the tape undecipherable. In addition, many portable cassette machines use dc biasing. This is noisy, and random spikes during the absence of tone may be interpreted as tone, unless special precautions are taken.

Because of the many disadvantages, this method is no longer used, although it may be encountered in old equipment.

Pulse Ratio Encoding

Records a 1 as a tone burst lasting more than half the bit time and a 0 as a tone burst lasting less than half the bit time. A single tone may be turned on or off (Figure 10.1B), or two tones may be used. A practical ratio is obtained when the *mark* tone lasts for one-third of the bit time (logic 0) or two-thirds of the bit time (logic 1), as shown in Figure 10.1B.

A single tone makes the method vulnerable to noise, but since a bit clock can be recovered from the tape, speed variations of up to 20 percent are tolerated. For data rates up to 300 bits per second, the hardware interface can be extremely simple, all detection of bit cell boundaries being performed by software.

Dual tones and hardware separation of clock and data pulses improve the reliability. The data rate is limited by the number of cycles required by the filters to separate the two tones, but a data rate of 800 bits per second is not difficult to obtain. Tones in the 6,000- to 8,000-hertz range, with phase-locked loop detectors which respond very quickly, yield data rates of 2,500 bits per second. Higher data rates can seldom be obtained with audio tapes and drives, because the medium and the tape speed limit the number of flux transitions per linear inch.

Frequency-Shift Keying

Two frequencies are recorded: one represents a logic 1 and the other (usually the lower) represents a logic 0, (Figure 10.1C). There are no unrecorded gaps except between files, so that tape noise is less of a

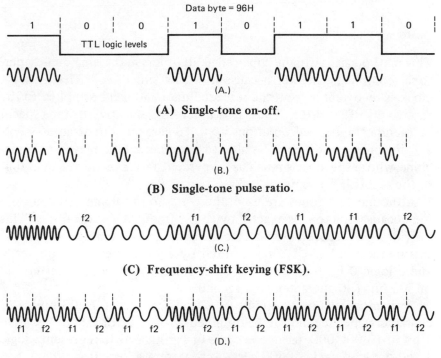

(A) Single-tone on-off.

(B) Single-tone pulse ratio.

(C) Frequency-shift keying (FSK).

(D) Dual-tone phase encoding.

Figure 10.1. Analog recording methods.

problem. The method is still speed-sensitive, because the receive bit clock is generated on the interface board, at a fixed rate in expectation of a fixed linear tape speed.

Further, if the two tones are closely spaced in pitch, sharp filters are needed to separate them. This increases the speed sensitivity; speed variations from the recording machine to the playback machine, or speed drift within the length of a single tape, tend to move the recovered tones onto the skirts of the filter response and thereby reduce the output amplitudes. If the tones are more widely spaced in pitch, then the filters need not be so sharp and speed sensitivity is reduced. However, care must be taken to ensure that harmonics of the lower frequency do not produce spurious responses from the filter turned to the upper frequency. Several well-designed interfaces using this method are on the market. They are reliable at transfer rates between 300 and 600 bits per second—the latter with slightly increased error rate.

Dual-Tone Phase Encoding

This method has virtually superseded all others in the high-quality personal computing market because it is "self-clocking." That is, a bit clock is recoverable from the recorded data and can be applied to the receiving shift register. Thus, it is much less sensitive to tape speed. It tolerates tape-speed variations up to 16 percent with no adjustment; and in some cases it may be able to decipher a tape played on a machine whose speed is as much as 20 percent faster or slower than that of the recording machine.

Although two tones are used, there are no problems with harmonics, because one tone is exactly twice the frequency of the other. This provides the recoverable bit clock. In the most common version of this method, a logic 1 is represented by eight cycles of 2,400 hertz, and a logic 0 by four cycles of 1,200 hertz to provide a transfer rate of 300 bits (30 characters) per second.

With more elaborate circuitry, a transfer rate of 1,200 bits (120 characters) per second can be obtained with an error rate of less than 1 bit in 10,000,000, using one cycle of 1,200 hertz to represent a logic 1 and one-half cycle of 600 hertz to represent a logic 0.

Synchronous and Asynchronous Recording

Audio tape and cassette interfaces designed for data transfer rates up to 1,200 bits per second use an asynchronous serializer/deserializer between the analog circuits and the computer data bus such as a UART (*Universal Asynchronous Receiver/Transmitter*) telecommunications chip. The serializer on the chip converts a parallel byte from the CPU to a group of eight serial bits for recording; the deserializer accepts a serial bit stream from the analog interface and assembles bytes for the CPU.

When the interface is active but no data is provided by the CPU, the UART produces a constant logic 1 level which is recorded as a mark tone. Each byte to be written (8 data bits) is framed by a start bit consisting of a logic 0 level for one bit time (converted to a space tone); and a stop bit consisting of a logic 1 level for one bit time (converted to a mark tone). Thus, each CPU byte produces 10 bits; this accounts for the conversion factor of 10 so that 30 characters per second is equivalent to 300 bits per second.

Bits are timed in and out by a bit clock that is generated on the interface board during recording or recovered from the tape during playback. Since the beginning and end of each byte read is clearly identified by the start and stop bits, the interval between bytes is unimportant; each byte can be correctly deserialized as it arrives from the tape. This has the advantage that blocks of data can be of any length. If one clock bit is missed because of tape or system noise, only the byte in which it occurs is affected, the bytes following are correctly received. The penalty is the additional two synchronizing bits for each data byte.

Data density is increased by 20 percent by omitting the start and stop bits. A missed clock pulse now scrambles all the following bytes. For this reason, data blocks without synchronizing bits are usually limited to 255 bytes. The serializer/deserializer is a USART (Universal Synchronous/Asynchronous Receiver Transmitter) which can also be used for asynchronous transmissions but is more expensive than a UART.

The synchronous idle condition is a series of 8-bit characters. The ASCII SYN character (binary 00010110) is standard in telecommunications, but cassette systems sometimes use another character (such as 01101110). The USART deserializer circuits can identify the beginning and end of this pattern and become synchronized within eight bit times. Once the sync character is identified, the beginning and end of the following bytes is derived by simply counting groups of 8 bits. However, it is impossible to retain synchronism indefinitely; further, an error in any one bit requires retransmission of the entire block. For a block length of 256 bytes, the bit-sampling point at the receiver remains well within allowable tolerances, and retransmission of the block after an error does not entail excessive overhead. Also, this number is easy to count in microcomputers with 8-bit registers. Thus, 256 bytes is the normal block length in microcomputer cassette systems with synchronous data transfer.

Effect of Waveshape

Audio tape and cassette drives have a response range of 20 to 20,000 hertz for high-quality units, and 50 to 9,000 hertz for inexpensive units. A signal recorded at constant amplitude and swept over the entire range does not have a constant amplitude at the output of the playback head. This is because head inductance and gap-width effects cause the response to rise at a rate of 6 decibels per octave in the range 20 to 400 hertz and to drop off very rapidly when the signal wavelength is less than the gap width of the playback head. A typical frequency/amplitude response curve for a playback head is shown in Figure 10.2. To obtain a flat response over the whole range, the record electronics boost the signal level for frequencies above 1,000

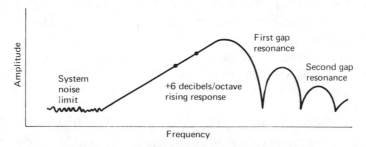

Figure 10.2.   Response of a tape playback
head to a constant amplitude recording.

hertz, and the playback electronics boost its frequencies below 400 hertz.

As the result of the compensation applied during recording and playback, audio units do not take kindly to the square waves required for digital circuits. A square wave (Figure 10.3A) recorded on a low-cost cassette is highly distorted, emerging from the playback circuits looking something like Figure 10.3B, which is difficult to demodulate successfully. If the square wave is routed through a low-pass filter so that the recorded waveshape resembles Figure 10.3C, the playback response will be more like Figure 10.3D, which is usable.

Much depends upon the design of the analog decoder. Some decoders for FSK (frequency-shift keying) or dual-tone phase encoding are sensitive to differences in amplitude between the two tones even though tolerant of frequency variations. Careful adjustment of the playback volume and tone controls may be necessary for reliable recovery of digital data. And, certain inexpensive cassette units handle digital data at speeds up to 1,200 bits per second much better than some of the more costly high-quality units.

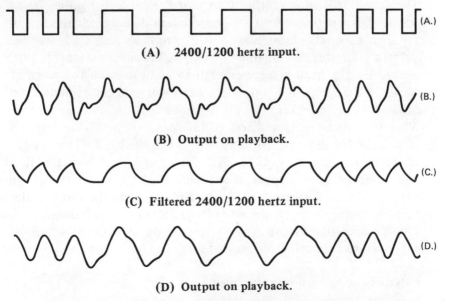

(A)   2400/1200 hertz input.

(B) Output on playback.

(C) Filtered 2400/1200 hertz input.

(D) Output on playback.

Figure 10. 3. Recording and playback waveshapes.

10.2 DIGITAL RECORDING METHODS

The audio recording methods described are suitable for data rates up to about 2,400 bits per second. Transfer rates above this require different techniques. Data density is a function of the magnetic characteristics of the medium and the head design. The material, its granularity, the width of the head gap and the distance of the head from the medium are among the factors which impose a limit to the number of flux changes that can be distinguished on the medium.

Data transfer speed is a function of the velocity of the medium past the record/play head and of the maximum flux changes per inch. Audio tape velocity is standard industry-wide. Open-reel or cartridge drives run at speeds from 3.75 inches per second up through 120 inches per second, whereas the standard speed for capstan-driven cassettes is 1.825 inches per second. There are no standards for hub-driven cassettes. Eight-inch floppy disks rotate at a standard speed of 360 revolutions per minute. Thus, to obtain the fastest transfer rate for a particular type of drive, the problem is to pack as many data bits as possible onto the medium without exceeding the flux-changes-per inch limit.

The audio recording methods are not designed to handle narrow pulses at high repetition rates. Increased data density is achieved with heads having a smaller inductance and electronics which apply a square wave that saturates the medium. That is, the magnetomotive force generated by the head is large enough to align most of the magnetic particles in the neighborhood of the head gap, and the remanence of the recording material keeps them aligned.

When unidirectionally magnetized tape passes beneath the playback head, a constant magnetic field is induced in the head. The head responds only to a change in field. When magnetic particles magnetized in the other direction appear, the direction of the magnetic field in the core is reversed abruptly. The core responds to the rapid change in flux to produce a sharp output voltage pulse in the winding.

The bit encoding methods most commonly used on cassette, cartridge, open-reel tape and disk drives are:

- NRZI (nonreturn to zero, ones).
- Frequency modulation (FM).

- Modified frequency modulation (MFM).
- Modified modified frequency modulation (MMFM).
- Group-coded recording (GCR).

In discussing the signals associated with these encoding methods, we distinguish between *timing* elements that delimit and count bit cells and *data* elements that represent 1s or 0s. Bit streams are sometimes illustrated (as in Figure 10.4A) with a clock pulse at the leading edge of a bit cell and a data pulse in the middle of a cell. In practice, neither element is actually a "pulse," which by definition has two signal level transitions that produce two flux reversals. Rather, the presence of a timing element is represented by a single flux reversal. A data 1 may be represented by a flux in one direction or by a flux reversal and a data 0 by a flux in the other direction or the absence of a flux reversal, according to the encoding method.

NRZI

This method (Figure 10.4B) is seldom used for high-density tapes, and never for floppy or hard disks, but it is found in some digital cassette drives. It consists of magnetizing a bit cell to saturation in one direction for a 1 and in the other direction for a 0. The method has several disadvantages. First, it is not self-clocking; that is, a clock pulse is not directly recoverable from the bit stream. Some devices generate the receiver bit clock locally on the interface board, but more often clock pulses are recorded on a separate track. Second, the method requires a bandwidth from dc to the data rate because long strings of 0s or 1s create no flux change. The signal then contains a large dc component which may drift with time and require compensating circuitry in the playback electronics.

Frequency Modulation (FM)

The FM technique uses a single track and writes a clock transition at the beginning of every bit cell. As shown in Figure 10.4C, a data

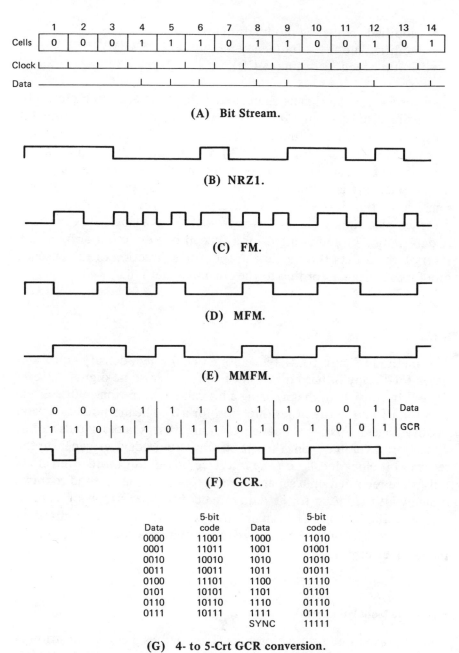

(A) Bit Stream.

(B) NRZ1.

(C) FM.

(D) MFM.

(E) MMFM.

(F) GCR.

Data	5-bit code	Data	5-bit code
0000	11001	1000	11010
0001	11011	1001	01001
0010	10010	1010	01010
0011	10011	1011	01011
0100	11101	1100	11110
0101	10101	1101	01101
0110	10110	1110	01110
0111	10111	1111	01111
		SYNC	11111

(G)   4- to 5-Crt GCR conversion.

Figure 10.4. Digital bit encoding methods.

transition is present in the middle of the bit cell if the cell contains a 1 and is absent if the cell contains a 0. The clock transition tells the controller that in time $T/2$ it should look for a data transition. A clock transition at the beginning of each cell, regardless of cell contents, ensures proper timing with simple circuitry. FM is not as efficient as some other techniques, since clock transitions are always present; thus, it does not make the best use of the flux-changes-per-inch limit. Nevertheless, it is satisfactory for densities up to 6,400 flux-changes-per-inch, and at the standard floppy disk rotation speed of 360 revolutions per minute yeilds a data transfer rate of 250,000 bits per second. An IBM 3740-compatible diskette with 77 tracks and 26 sectors per track has a formatted capacity of 256,256 bytes.

Modified Frequency Modulation (MFM)

MFM, for which a sample pulse train is shown in Figure 10.4D, is an encoding method that significantly increases the capacity of the medium (floppy disk). To encode a 1, it changes the direction of magnetization in the middle of the bit cell but omits the clock transition from the start of the cell. For a 0 bounded by two 1s, it omits both the data transition and the clock transition. For a 0 preceded by another 0, it writes a clock transition at the start of the bit cell but no data transition. This method doubles the data density without greatly increasing circuit complexity.

Modified MFM (MMFM)

This type of encoding, shown in Figure 10.4E, further reduces the average number of flux reversals per message. MMFM puts a clock transition at the leading edge of a 0 cell only if the previous cell contains neither a data transition nor a clock transition. In the example, we see that a clock transition is required at the start of cell 2, since the clock transition was omitted from cell 1 (because cell 0 contained a data transition). However, the presence of a clock transition in cell 2 allows the clock transition to be omitted from cell 3.

Compared to FM, the MFM and MMFM encoding methods halve the number of flux changes per linear track inch for the same number of bit cells and transfer rate. Thus, by doubling the transfer rate, the amount of data packed per linear track inch is doubled with practically no increase in the number of flux changes. Little change to the software driver is needed if we keep the number of sectors per track constant: there are now 256 instead of 128 bytes per sector and we need only enlarge the one-sector read/write memory buffer to 256 bytes. Alternatively, we might keep the sector length at 128 bytes and double the number of sectors per track. Using MFM, the extra space for sector headers limits us to 51 sectors; with the greater bit density of MMFM, however, we can record up to 58 sectors per track in this way.

Group-Coded Recording (GCR)

In the GCR method, no more than two 0s are recorded in succession, which makes it easier to retain synchronism. Also, successive transitions are 1 bit time apart, so that the allowable shift rises from 0.25-bit time to 0.5-bit time. The bandwidth needed is from 0.33f to f (where f is the data rate); for NRZ it is dc to f; and for FM it is f to 2f.

GCR avoids encoding more than two successive 0s by translating 4 data bits into 5 recorded bits, which give 32 possible patterns. Of these, we discard all which begin or end with more than one 0, and all that contain more than two successive 0s internally. This leaves us with 17 usable patterns; 16 of these can represent the 16 possible 4-bit data patterns and the sevententh (111111) is reserved as a synchronization pattern. The most common translation table is shown in Figure 10.4G. The waveform is shown in Figure 10.4F.

This method of encoding offers the same data density as does MMFM, at the cost of some increase in hardware complexity, but with a narrower bandwidth and increased reliability owing to a larger timing margin. Consider that on an IBM-compatible diskette, operating in single density at 250,000 bits per second, the minimum nominal time between flux changes for FM is one-half the bit time, or 2 microseconds. For reliable decoding, the sampling of transitions should not be displaced by more than half this time (±1 microsecond). If we now double the data rate, the drift allowed is only ±0.5 microsecond, or about 19 microinches on the innermost track.

11
Cassette and Cartridge Drives

11.1 CASSETTE DRIVES

Cassette drives used with microcomputer systems and with some type-writer or CRT terminals are of three types:

- Standard audio cassette machines, where record/play and fast-forward/rewind modes are set manually, but the computer turns the drive motor on or off.
- Digital cassette drives, where the record/play mode and all tape motion are controlled by the computer.
- Digital incremental drives where tape motion is accomplished by a stepping motor which steps once for each character delivered and is controlled from the computer.

Audio cassette drives are used in low-cost personal computer systems where medium speed and serial access are tolerable.

Fully controllable digital cassettes are found in higher-priced personal computer systems, to provide higher data density, faster data transfer and full computer control. Their applications include:

- Dedicated systems for monitoring communication lines.
- Remote collection and transmission of analog data.
- Backup for floppy and minifloppy disks.

The incremental digital cassette drive is found in the key-to-tape terminal where text editing is done off-line. Edited text written by the terminal on the cassette is later submitted to the host computer. The incremental drive allows backspacing to replace as little as a single character on the tape. Off-line editing is valuable for time-sharing communications terminals to reduce connect time and charges. Terminals no longer incorporate incremental cassette drives now that floppy disk facilities are cheaper, although many are still found in the field.

Audio Cassette Drives

Personal computing systems that use cassettes as their external storage do not always have a dedicated cassette drive for program and data storage; it may be detached from the computer to record music and speech. Even if a drive is purchased specifically for computer use, it is likely to be an inexpensive model audio cassette. Interface designs therefore have the following constraints:

- The cassette unit must be usable without alteration.
- Speed variations of 10 percent are encountered when playing on one machine a tape that was recorded on another machine.
- Variations in frequency response are encountered between different drives and between different brands of tape. Some tape drives have tone controls that may help to obtain usable digital signals in spite of these variations.

Connections to the cassette drive consist of standard audio shielded cables, with miniature or subminature plugs at one end to mate with the MIC and PHONE (or AUX and MON) jacks on the drive. Similar connectors are generally used at the computer end also, although multipin connectors are sometimes used on interfaces that plug into the S-100 bus. If the interface provides motor control, two wires for motor control may also be present. At one end a subminiature plug mates with the *remote* jack on the drive; at the computer end, the wires go to the contacts of a motor control relay, if motor control is provided. Since the recorder is connected without modification, it is necessary to use audio signals to record digital data. Several methods are available to do this:

- Single tone on/off.
- Frequency shift keying (FSK).
- Phase encoding.

Digital Cassette Drives

A number of manufacturers supply computer-controlled digital cassette drives; Raymond, Quantex, and ICP are among the best known. Some drives have a capstan to drive the tape past the record/playback head at constant speed. More usually, the take-up hub is driven at a constant speed. In the latter case, with constant angular velocity, tape speed increases as the hub fills with tape. Since a bit clock is always recoverable from the tape, the speed change is of little consequence. Some drive units use a single motor with a friction drive linkage that engages either the forward hub or the reverse hub under solenoid control. Other units have two motors, one for each hub.

Unlike audio units, digital units do not lift the tape away from the read/write head during fast spooling. This provides detection of interrecord gaps during fast forward or fast reverse. Reading or writing is done in either direction, but at normal speed. Thus, with appropriate software, high-speed searches can be conducted for a particular file or block.

Digital cassette drives do not have erase heads, nor do they use dc or high-frequency bias. Instead, saturation recording is used: to record a 1, a constant current is applied to the read/write head to saturate the tape in one direction; to write a 0, the current is reversed to saturate the tape with the opposite polarity.

The same head that records the digital signals reads them on playback. The head output voltage is proportional to the rate of change of magnetic flux, and transitions from 0 to 1 generate an electrical pulse in one direction; transitions from 1 to 0 generate pulses in the other direction. A continuous series of 1s (or 0s) produces no transitions, and therefore (because the flux is constant) produces no pulses except at the start and end of the series.

Saturation recording is reliable and largely insensitive to noise, because the output pulses generated by transitions are relatively large. Depending on head design, tape composition and tape speed, pulses may reach peak amplitudes of 5 to 10 millivolts. In audio machines the peak-to-peak signal level at the head seldom exceeds 1 millivolt at 400 hertz, and decreases by 6 decibels per octave below 200 hertz, where the rate of flux change is reduced, and by 10 decibels per octave at high frequencies where the wavelength of the signal is less than the gap width of the playback head.

The nature of saturation recording, which generates detectable signals only at transitions from 0 to 1, or vice versa, requires a recoverable bit clock (delimiting cell boundaries) for reliable reading at high data rates. This is done with:

- Separate tracks for data and clock pulses.
- A single track for both.

Since data density is a function of the allowable flux changes per linear track inch, the clock rate is usually set at half the data rate when using a separate clock track. As a result, clock transitions occur at the leading edge of a bit cell, while data transitions, when present, appear in the middle.

Recording clock and data pulses on the same track requires more complex circuitry, but allows efficient encoding methods such as MFM, MMFM and GCR (described in Chapter 10). Data rates of 9,600 bits per second or more can be obtained with these methods.

Incremental Cassettes

Incremental cassette units use saturation recording but a stepping motor controls the tape motion. For reliability and simplicity, data is on one track and clock pulses on another. There are large gaps between bytes to allow a single byte to be rerecorded without destroying those on each side of it; this limits the data transfer rate to 300 bits per second.

11.2 CASSETTE/COMPUTER INTERFACE

A typical cassette/computer interface, shown in the block diagram of Figure 11.1, has five main sections:

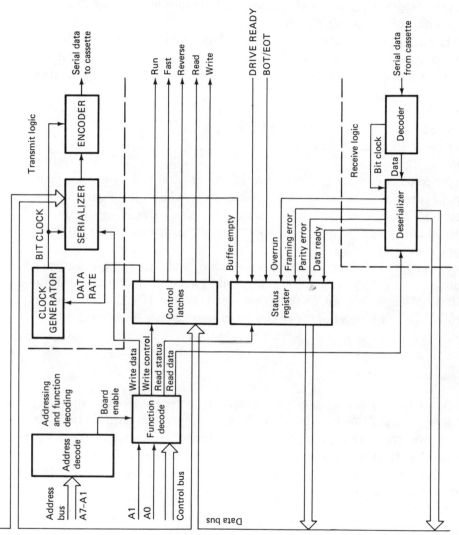

Figure 11.1.   Cassette interface; block diagram.

- Device addressing and function decoding.
- Control logic.
- Status register.
- Transmit logic.
- Receive logic.

Device Addressing and Function Decoding

Four device addresses are allocated to the cassette interface. The address used depends on the function requested:

- Writing data to tape.
- Reading data from tape.
- Sending drive control commands.
- Interrogating drive and transmit/receive status.

The tape drive address decoder examines the six high-order address bits (14 for memory-mapped I/O) to generate a board enable signal. (For details, refer to Chapter 1.) The two low-order address bits distinguish the four device addresses (or functions). The selected address is combined with timing and control signals from the CPU to produce one of the four cassette control signals: write, data, read data, read status and write control.

Control Logic

The write control signal loads 8 bits in parallel from the data bus into the control register. Each bit enables or disables (1 or 0) one function: e.g., one bit initializes the transmit/receive logic; another determines the data rate of the transmit section: others control the speed and direction of tape motion.

Recall that the digital cassette drive is completely controllable by the computer. Remote control of functions is found only on luxury audio cassette drives. On cheaper models, the drive is manually placed in forward; the control logic only turns the motor on and off to start or stop the tape. Because the motor has no braking when turned off, and also takes 2 to 4 seconds to come up to speed after power is applied, the software drivers customarily provide long interrecord gaps.

All rewind and fast-forward operations are manually performed on these drives.

Status Logic

The single status register shown in Figure 11.1 may be the transmit/receive status register that is an integral part of a UART (Universal Asynchronous Transmitter-Receiver) or USART (Universal Synchronous/Asynchronous Receiver-Transmitter) chip, together with other small registers independently gated onto specific lines of the data bus. Minimum requirements for an audio cassette are:

- A buffer empty bit.
- A data ready bit.

The buffer empty bit indicates that the transmitter section is ready to accept a new character; the data ready bit indicates that a character has been received and assembled in the receiver section.

UARTs and USARTs indicate parity, framing and overrun error conditions with flags (see Chapter 1). These three flags are seldom examined by audio cassette drivers. Instead, the software usually performs checksum of Cyclic Redundancy (CRC) checking, which is more effective than a simple parity check; these methods detect multiple-bit errors within a single character and lost characters.

The digital cassette driver examines the drive ready (power is on and cassette is mounted), EOT (end-of-tape) and/or BOT (beginning-of tape) signals from the drive.

One way to detect BOT and EOT is with a strip of conducting foil cemented to the outer surface of the tape at each end of the recording medium. The detector is a pair of insulated metallic posts over which the tape passes, thereby providing a conducting path between the two posts through the foil. More often, the last 8 to 10 inches of the tape consist of clear leader—that is, tape base with no magnetic coating. The detector is a photocell; a lamp is on the other side of the tape. When the photocell is activated by light passing through the clear leader, it generates a signal.

When the foil strip (or clear leader) is detected, the status of the last direction command encountered indicates whether we are at the beginning or the end of the tape. This determination may be done by software. If the last direction command was forward, the detected signal is interpreted as EOT; if the direction was reverse, then the signal is interpreted as BOT. A time-out is also provided in case a forward command was given when the tape was already at the end, or a reverse command when it was at the beginning. Under these conditions the tape cannot move, since it is pulling against the empty hub to which it is attached; if no timeout is provided, the driver routine will wait indefinitely for the signal, indicating that the opposite end of the tape has been reached. When the system cannot proceed because of some error like this, it is said to "hang up."

Transmit Logic

The transmit section of the interface board consists of a clock generator, a serializer and an encoder. UARTs normally require a clock that is 16 times the data rate, but USARTs and other programmable serializers allow the external clock to be divided by 64, 16 and 1, so that the program can set three different data rates. The serializer is usually part of a UART or USART chip; it consists of a one-character parallel-in, parallel-out buffer, and a parallel-in, serial-out shift register. When both registers are empty, the buffer empty flag is set. A character presented by the CPU is loaded first into the buffer and then immediately afterward into the shift register; the buffer empty flag remains high. If the CPU presents a second character while the first one is still being shifted out of the shift register, it is loaded into the buffer and the buffer empty flag goes down. The driver then waits for the buffer empty flag to go high again before presenting another character. When the shift register is empty, the character waiting in the buffer is immediately transferred to the shift register and the buffer empty flag is set.

The encoder converts the serial bit stream coming from the shift register into audio tones (in two-tone FSK systems), or to a bit stream containing both data and clock pulses (for audio phase encoding and most saturation recording methods). The encoded clock is derived from the 16-times bit clock applied to the serializer.

Receive Logic

The receive section of the interface board is the inverse of the transmit section. The decoder for FSK or phase-encoded systems converts audio signals from the drive into digital signals. If the bit stream also contains clock pulses, these are extracted and applied separately to the shift register of the deserializer—a shift register and a one-character buffer. A character assembled in the shift register is immediately transferred to the output buffer and the data ready flag is set. The shift register can then begin assembling the following character. When the CPU issues a read data command, the read data signal generated on the interface board gates the output buffer onto the data bus and also resets the data ready flag. If the receive driver reads the buffer when the data ready flag is inactive, it finds either garbage or the last character assembled (which has not yet been replaced by a new character from the shift register). If the driver waits too long, the character in the buffer is overwritten by the next character from the shift register, and hence is lost. The overrun error flag is set when this happens. Overrun errors can be avoided by ensuring that the driver frequently interrogates the data ready flag and reads the data register immediately after it finds the flag set.

12
Disk Drives

12.1 PHYSICAL STRUCTURE OF DISKETTE

The diskette, now generally referred to as a "floppy disk," was originally introduced by IBM as a rapid means of loading microprogramming information into the System/370 CPU. A standard storage layout of the diskette was also developed by IBM. Diskettes which use this general layout are called "IBM-compatible." Actually, differences in file structure make it improbable that such a diskette could be processed by an IBM system.

Other applications for this fast, reliable storage medium were soon found, and at the time of writing it and its smaller brother, the minifloppy, are the principal external storage media in microcomputer systems where rapid random access to data is required.

The diskette (Figure 12.1) consists of a circular, flexible, plastic base, uniformly coated on both sides with magnetic material similar to that used for magnetic tapes. To protect the recording surface, the diskette is enclosed in a thin plastic liner which has a very low coefficient of friction to permit the diskette to rotate easily within, and also to help clean the surface. An outer jacket of thin cardboard treated with antistatic material surrounds the combination to provide physical protection from abrasion. A radial window through the jacket and liner allows the read/write head of the diskette drive to come into direct contact with the recording surface.

A smaller circular window in the package allows the free passage of light when an index hole in the diskette proper passes under the window; a photocell mounted on the drive detects this light and converts it to an electrical pulse that signals the start of a recording track.

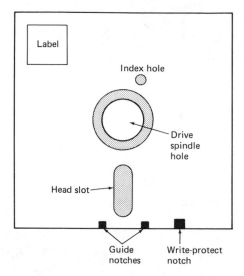

Figure 12.1. External appearance of floppy disk.

Two small notches in the bottom edge engage with guides on the drive frame to ensure that the diskette is correctly positioned with the central hole over the spindle. A larger notch, when present, allows light to reach a photocell that generates a write-protect signal. Data can read from an 8-inch disk with this notch, but cannot be written to it. If the notch is not present, or if the user covers it with opaque tape, the diskette is write-enabled. For minifloppies, the reverse convention is standard; a diskette is write-protected when the notch is covered.

The diskette is inserted into the drive through the rectangular opening in the front of the case. Closing the door pushes the diskette down over the drive spindle and engages a pressure clutch that presses the diskette firmly against a plate mounted on the rotating spindle. This starts the diskette rotating inside its jacket. The drive mechanism is described in more detail later in this chapter.

12.2 DATA STORAGE LAYOUT

Tracks

Data are stored as a serial bit stream on discrete, concentric tracks on the diskette (see Figure 12.2). A standard 8-inch diskette has 77 such

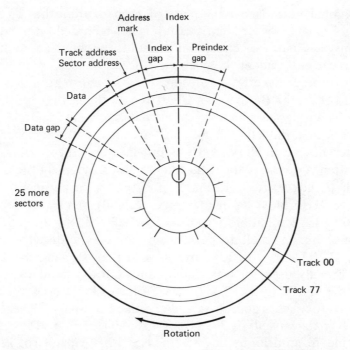

Figure 12.2. Tracks and sectors on IBM-compatible diskette.

tracks, numbered 00 (outermost) through 76 (innermost) and sep-
arated by blank "guard bands." The software can request the drive
to position the read/write head over any specified track. When the
index hole in the diskette passes under the jacket window, the index
detector photocell generates a brief pulse to signal that the start of a
recording track is about to pass under the read/write head position.
This is valid for any track above which the head is positioned.

Sectors

Each of the 77 tracks is divided into sectors; one sector (128 data
bytes in the IBM format) is the smallest amount of data that can be
transferred in response to a software read or write command. The two
methods of identifying sectors within a track are called *hard-sectoring*
and *soft-sectoring*. Hard-sectored diskettes have one index hole that
signals the start of a track and hence the first sector. Thirty-one small-

er additional holes signal the start of each of the other sectors. A machine-readable sector identification is not recorded on the diskette itself; instead, hardware circuits in the controller keep count of which sector is currently under the read/write head.

Soft-sectored diskettes have only the one index hole that signals the start of track. Before data is written to them, they must be formatted by a program which writes the data shown in Figure 12.3 onto each track in turn. The "data fields" are filled with the hexadecimal character E5; when the diskette is put into use, these fields will be overwritten by user's data. The track address byte is in the range 00 through 4C hex (0 to 77 decimal), and the sector address byte is in the range 01 through 1A hex (1 to 26 cecimal). Thus, the data capacity of an IBM-compatible diskette is $77 \times 26 \times 128 = 256,256$ bytes. It is, of course, possible to pack more data on the diskette by using sectors of 1024 or even 2048 bytes, with a consequent saving of the space normally used for sector addressing, but the standard format is 26 sectors of 128 bytes. The hard-sectored diskette does not require any space for sector addresses, and can therefore pack 32 sectors per track. Its data capacity is $77 \times 32 \times 128 = 315,392$ bytes.

A standard minifloppy has 35 tracks, with a capacity of 110 kilobytes unformatted, or about 89 kilobytes when formatted into 128-byte sectors. The 8-inch soft-sectored IBM format is the only industry-wide standard. Some 5-1/4-inch drives have 40 or more tracks, and methods of formatting double-density vary from one controller manufacturer to another.

Choice of Sectoring Methods

The choice of sector-identification method depends to a large extent on the importance given by the user to software portability. Hard sectoring allows more data to be put on the disk; however, there are two standards which are incompatible:

- Shugart drives require the sector holes to be inside the recorded tracks.
- Memorex drives require the sector holes to be outside the recorded tracks.
- Neither type can read soft-sectored diskettes.

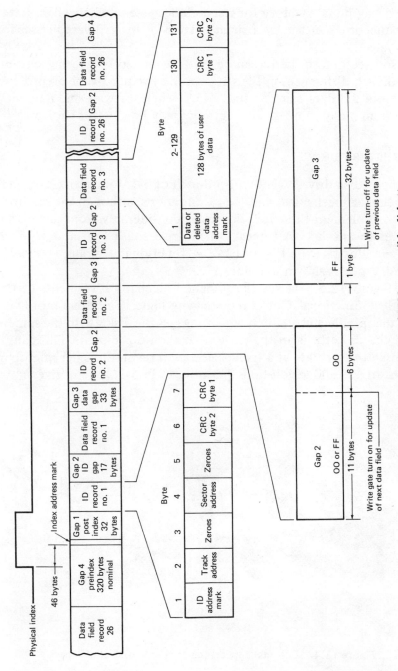

Figure 12.3.   3-track format of IBM-compatible diskette.

This may be satisfactory for stand-alone systems where all diskettes will be recorded either by a single system or by software houses for that system.

A soft-sectored diskette can be read by any soft-sectoring system, even though differences in file structure may require some preprocessing before the data can be used. Thus, when software and data may come from many sources, soft-sectoring may be a better choice.

12.3 THE DISK DRIVE

All floppy-disk drives, whether for 8-inch or 5-1/4-inch diskettes, perform similar mechanical and logical functions, although the methods used to implement these functions vary considerably from one manufacturer to another. A typical 8-inch drive and a typical 5-1/4-inch drive are illustrated in Figure 12.4. A functional diagram, applicable to both types, is shown in Figure 12.5.

In Figure 12.5 you see the principal mechanical elements of the drive and functional blocks representing logic. The drive motor rotates the spindle and a clutch which engages the diskette to the spindle when the diskette is in the drive with the door closed. This causes the diskette to rotate at a fixed speed (360 revolutions per minute in 8-inch drives, 300 revolutions per minute in 5-1/4-inch drives). An

Figure 12.4. External appearance of floppy and minifloppy.

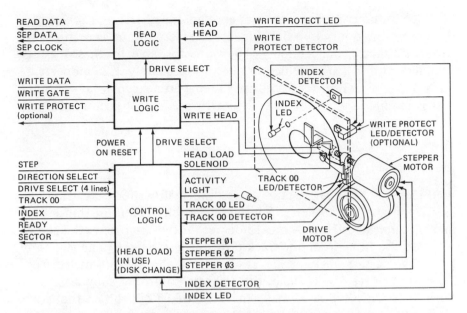

Figure 12.5. Floppy disk drive; functional diagram.

interlock switch on the door causes the control logic to generate the READY signal only when the door is closed and the diskette has completed two revolutions. Minifloppy drives do not generate a READY signal, but if the controller requires one, it can be generated by extra circuitry that counts two INDEX pulses, loads the head and then waits for the 75-millisecond head-load delay before activating the READY line. On 8-inch drives, there is a release bar which is pressed to open the door and eject the diskette by spring pressure. On 5-1/4-inch drives, there is no door. A snap bar, which does not completely close the opening, holds the diskette in place and activates the interlock switch. The activity light is normally located in the center of the release bar on 8-inch drives, and below the diskette opening on 5-1/4-inch drives.

Drive Motor

The drive motor in an 8-inch drive is a synchronous ac motor which requires approximately 0.4 amperes at 115 VAC, and turns the diskette continuously when power is applied and the clutch is engaged by closing the door. In a 5-1/4-inch drive, less torque is required to turn the diskette, and economy of power is desirable; for these reasons a smaller motor is used which draws approximately 1.25 amperes at 12 VDC. The motor does not turn the diskette except when disk access is required; when the drive is not in use, motor power is turned off.

Head Positioning

A three-phase stepper motor moves the read/write head assembly radially across the diskette. The most common motion translation mechanism is a lead screw; one 15-degree motor step rotates this screw to move the head from one track position to the next. The standard track spacing is 48 tracks per inch for both 8-inch and 5-1/4-inch drives. To move the read/write head, the diskette controller supplies a DI—RECTION SELECT level and a number of STEP pulses; the drive electronics apply these signals to a 3-bit up/down counter whose outputs are applied to the stepper motor via the STEPPER 01, STEPPER 02 and STEPPER 03 lines. Only one of these lines is active (low) at a time. When stepping in, the sequence is 1-2-3-1; when stepping out, it is 1-3-2-1.

Initialization

For diskette subsystem initialization on power-up and on system RESET, the head should go to track 00. An LED and photocell detector are positioned so as to generate the TRACK 00 signal when the read/write head is positioned over the outermost track on the diskette. For RESET, the controller generates an outward DIRECTION SELECT level and then pulses the STEP line until the TRACK 00 line goes high.

The index LED and detector photocell are mounted on opposite sides of the diskette over the circular index window of the jacket. Whenever the index hole in the diskette passes under the window, the detector generates a signal which is translated by the control electronics into a square INDEX pulse.

Write Protect

The write-protect LED and detector photocell are found on opposite sides of the diskette jacket, over the write-protect notch position. If the notch is present in the jacket, the detector generates a signal which is translated to a TTL (Transistor-Transistor Logic) active-low WRITE-PROTECT signal. This internally inhibits writing and informs the controller that the diskette is protected. If the notch is absent, or has been masked, the WRITE-PROTECT signal is a TTL high, which tells the controller that writing is permitted.

Head Loading

The head load solenoid is inactive until a DRIVE SELECT signal is received from the diskette controller. Then the activity lamp lights and the head load solenoid is activated. The solenoid armature pushes down onto a flexible leaf spring mounted on the head assembly (Figure 12.6). This leaf spring has a pressure pad mounted on it, and pressure from this flexes the diskette slightly to bring the recording surface into light contact with the read/write head, which is mounted on a rigid support below the diskette.

Drive Selection

Four controller DRIVE SELECT lines are provided. In small systems, each of the four lines can be connected to a different drive; activating one of the lines causes the head to be loaded on the corresponding drive. If the system has more than four drives, jumpers on the drive control electronics board allow one of the DRIVE SELECT lines to

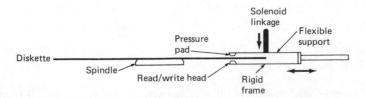

Figure 12.6.   Head load mechanism.

be used as a SELECT ENABLE line and the other three to be connected to a 1-of-8 decoder. In this configuration, up to eight drives can be handled by one controller.

Write

The write logic accepts a WRITE GATE level and WRITE DATA (data and clock) pulses from the controller. The WRITE GATE, when active, allows the data/clock pulses from the controller to enter the analog circuits that drive the write section of the read/write head. The diskette controller ensures that all conditions required for writing are satisfied before activating WRITE GATE and putting pulses on the WRITE DATA line. To write, we normally need:

- Drive ready (disk inserted and door closed).
- Diskette not protected.
- Head positioned over desired track.
- Desired sector identified.

Read

The read logic processes the waveform it receives from the read head and supplies a bit stream consisting of intermixed clock and data pulses on the READ DATA line (sometimes called the FD DATA line). Usually the controller is responsible for separating data and clock pulses and for regenerating clock pulses omitted in MFM and MMFM encoding. Some drive manufacturers, however, provide separation logic as an optional part of the read logic; in such cases the clock pulses (with missing pulses reinserted) appear on the SEP CLOCK line, and data pulses (for data cells representing a binary 1) appear on the SEP DATA line. When this option is implemented, the READ DATA line carrying the raw data is not used by the controller.

12.4 THE DISK CONTROLLER

The floppy-disk controller is the interface between the CPU and the drive, and sets or resets bits in a status register that can be read by the CPU. The status signals received from the drive include:

- READY (diskette mounted and rotating).
- Diskette protected/unprotected.
- TRACK 00 (head positioned over track 00).
- Others provided by the drive manufacturer.

The controller responds to the "primitives" listed below. Each primitive is a subroutine of the diskette driver package, performing one logical function. A primitive may contain many CPU instructions that implement its details.

- SELECT DRIVE activates one or more drive select line(s) to enable the specified drive in a multiple-drive system.
- HOME positions the head over track 00 and returns a TRACK 00 status signal to the operating system.
- TRACK SEEK causes the controller to position the head over a specified track.
- SET SECTOR loads the number of the desired sector into the controller sector register for a subsequent READ or WRITE command.
- SET DMA specifies the starting address of the memory buffer to be used by a subsequent read or write command.
- READ SECTOR reads the designated sector.
- WRITE SECTOR writes the designated sector.

The Home Command

This command is part of diskette drive initialization, and may be used whenever the software requires an indication of absolute diskette position before issuing relative track seek commands.

The Seek Command

If an LSI controller chip is in use, its track register contains the number of the current track, and the desired track number is placed in its data register. The controller compares the contents of the two registers and issues a direction signal—"out", if the data register value is smaller than the track register value, or "in" if the reverse is true. The controller then pulses the STEP line, updating the track register by one count for each pulse, until the contents of the two registers are equal. After moving the head, the controller reads the track address from the diskette. If this does not agree with the track address in the track register, an error status signal is returned to the CPU. The software may then issue a HOME command followed by a new TRACK SEEK command to move the head to the correct track. Disk controller boards which do not use an LSI controller chip maintain the current track number in memory and the software issues the step pulses to reach the desired track.

The set DMA Command

If the controller has a built-in DMA (direct-memory access) section, the buffer address and the byte count are loaded into hardware registers in the DMA section by separate commands. During a subsequent read or write operation, the DMA hardware preempts the system data bus and transfers a byte every time the diskette controller hardware makes a data request. The DMA hardware also preempts the address bus and increments the buffer address after every transfer.

If the controller does not have DMA circuitry, then programmed I/O transfers are performed. Now, the SET DMA command stores the address of a 128-byte buffer in a known memory location, and the read or write routine contains CPU instructions to update this pointer after each transfer. The byte count is maintained by the operating system; the user does not have to supply or update it.

The Read Sector Command

The controller compares the sector address in the sector register with each sector address read from the diskette. When a match is found, the next 128 bytes (user's data) and the two cyclic redundancy check (CRC) bytes for this sector are transferred via the data register to a memory buffer. If the CRC value computed during the read does not agree with the value in the two CRC bytes, the CRC error status bit is set as the command is terminated. The software will then usually make up to 10 further attempts to read the sector. If none of these succeed, a "hard error" or "permanent error" is reported to the operating system.

The Write Sector Command

The controller responds only if the drive supplies a READY signal (indicating that a diskette is mounted and that the door is closed) and a not protected signal. The software has supplied a TRACK SEEK and/or a HOME command, and a SET SECTOR command, to load the track and sector registers of the controller. The controller compares sector addresses read from the current track until the desired sector address is found; it then activates the write gate line and writes 128 bytes from the memory buffer to the user data area of this sector. While writing, the controller accumulates a 2-byte CRC value for the data and writes these 2 CRC bytes immediately after the last data byte. The write gate line is then deactivated to prevent any further writing.

Technology

Early models of floppy diskette controllers required 60 to 70 TTL and MSI (medium-scale integration) chips. As always, some trade-off between hardware and software was possible; fewer chips on a controller generally means more complex software and often some loss of speed. For example, when reading successive logical sectors, if the housekeeping took longer than the time for the next logical sector address to reach the head, the address mark would be missed and a full rotation of the diskette would be needed to bring it under the head again.

Today, most floppy diskette controllers use one LSI (large-scale integration) chip which contains logic for all controller functions and requires only I/O port address logic, some buffers, and drivers for the controller-to-drive output signals to complete the controller. Figure 12.7 shows the block diagram of a typical LSI floppy diskette controller chip—Western Digital's FD1771. Similar chips from other manufacturers are the Intel 8271 and the NEC MPD 372.

12.5 DISK CONTROLLER LOGIC

The computer interface portions of all I/O interface boards are similar. The diskette controller contains four separate diskette control

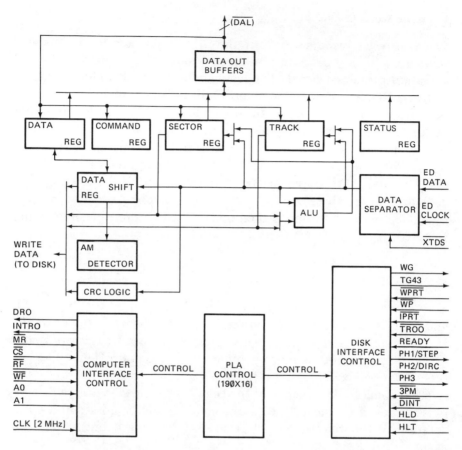

Figure 12.7. Floppy disk controller; block diagram.

ports selected by two address signals (A0 and A1), together with chip select and other signals that distinguish an I/O operation from a memory access. The computer interface returns a DRQ (data request) signal, used if DMA transfer is employed, an INTRQ (interrupt request) signal used by interrupt-driven systems, and status signals from the status register.

The floppy disk interface section accepts status signals from the drive and sends drive select, head load, direction and step signals to the drive. The LSI chip supplies little current, so external drivers boost this current to the drive; tristate buffers isolate the chip inputs from the drive. These drivers and buffers protect the delicate controller chip against electrical surges and noise spikes which might damage it.

Commands, status bytes and data are transferred between the CPU and the controller chip over the 8-bit computer data bus [labeled DAL (data access lines) in the diagram]. Commands from the CPU are loaded into the command register, which is enabled by one of the I/O ports in the computer interface control. A byte loaded into the command register is interpreted by the PLA (programmable logic array) section, which generates all timing and control signals required inside the chip, and results in appropriate signals to the drive.

When the operation is complete, bits are set or reset in the status register to indicate a successful operation or the type of error if the operation failed. The sector register and the track register are loaded by the CPU before any read, write or positioning operation except the HOME command. The data shift register converts parallel data held in the data register to serial format for writing to the disk, or assembles serial data from the diskette into a byte that is then transferred in parallel format to the CPU via the data register.

The data separator at the right of the diagram can be used for single-density drives, but since it is driven by the system clock, its resolution is not good enough to provide error rates better than 1 error in 10 million bits. To obtain better error rates, external separator logic is usually included on the board and is synchronized to the recorded clock during read operations and to a high-frequency crystal-controlled oscillator on the board during write operations.

The arithmetic/logic unit (ALU) usually can perform only comparing, incrementing and decrementing. It compares the contents of a register with a byte read from the diskette or the contents of two registers (e.g., the track and data registers during a track seek operation). It increments or decrements registers. Controller ALU operations are usually serial because one input is serial data from the diskette.

The address mark (AM) detector is a decoder that detects index marks (hex FC), ID address marks (hex FE) and data address marks (hex FB) during read and write operations.

The CRC logic generates or verifies the 16-bit cyclic redundancy check value that is written at the end of each ID or data field. The CRC is computed for all information in an ID or data field, starting with the address mark. It is capable of detecting multiple-bit errors in a single byte or multiple error bytes.

12.6 HARD DISKS

Disk drives which store 5 megabytes or more are called hard disk drives. The disk which make these up are rigid. A magnetic coating is deposited on a rigid substrate, usually an aluminum alloy. The disks rotate at 3,600 revolutions per minute. There are several standard disk diameters: 5-1/4 inches (for storage of 5 to 10 megabytes); 8 inches (for 10 to 30 megabytes); and 14 inches (for 30 megabytes or more). The Winchester technology for these drives was introduced by IBM for their 3340 disk drive, and has since been adopted by many other manufacturers. The drives consist of one or more platters (sometimes five); these are permanently mounted and cannot be removed by the user. (In development are removable hard disks using Winchester technology.)

In this head-per-surface drive, the heads are in contact with the medium when the power is off, while the disks are getting up to speed and when they are slowing down to a stop; however, they do not rest on the recorded portion of the platters. During normal operation, each read/write head floats on an air cushion approximately 45 microinches above the disk surface. The force lifting the head off the disk surface is created by air set rotating within the enclosure by friction between the air and the disk. The head carrier consists of three rail-like surfaces (Figure 12.8); the sloped leading edges of the rails create the aerodynamic lift. The read/write head is located at the trailing edge of the center rail.

Because the gap between the head and the medium is so small, it is essential to exclude dust and other foreign matter which could damage the head or the medium or both. Figure 12.9 shows the relative sizes of the air cushion and of various particles of comparable size. The velocity of the outer edge of the platter is about 150 miles per hour. Imagine the damage caused when the head crushes even a small particle against the disk. Precautions are taken during assembly to exclude all material particles from the assembly room; the drive operates in a hermetically sealed enclosure. Since the head is not in contact with the disk, it generates no heat. All heat-producing com-

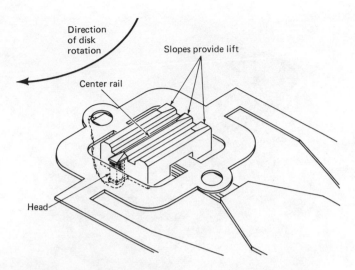

Figure 12.8.   Winchester head (for underside of disk).

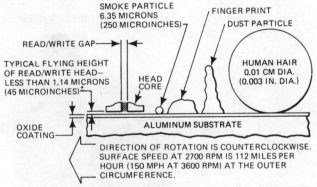

Figure 12.9.   Head flying height compared to foreign objects.

ponents are mounted outside the enclosure and are cooled either by convection or, in larger drives, by forced ventilation.

A typical dual-platter Winchester drive is shown in Figure 12.10. In Figure 12.11 the sealed cover has been removed to show the two platters, the head carrier and the drive that moves the heads across the platters. Figure 12.12 is a closeup view of one of the two head

Figure 12.10.   Voice coil drive. (Courtesy of Corvus Systems, Inc.)

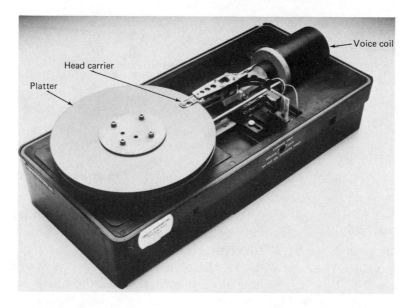

Figure 12.11.   Rotary head. (Courtesy of Corvus Systems, Inc.)

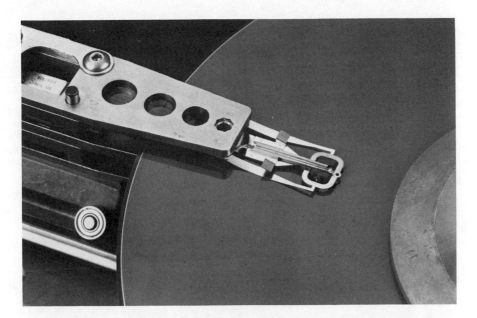

Figure 12.12.   Close-up of head carrier. (Courtesy of Corvus Systems, Inc.)

carriers. The head is moved across the platter by a voice-coil actuator, which consists of a wire coil mounted on a cylindrical former attached to the head carrier; the coil and its former slide between the poles of a powerful cylindrical magnet (seen at the right of Figure 12.11). The displacement of the solenoid from its home position is proportional to the current flowing through its coil, and is controlled by the analog portion of the disk controller. Conversion circuits translate a digital track seek request from the computer into a dc current that positions the head over the desired track.

Figure 12.13 shows another drive which uses a rotary servomotor; on this machine, the triangular structure at the rear of the drive rotates like a phonograph tone arm, moving the heads inward or outward over the platter. Linkages within the main structure maintain the tangential alignment of the heads over the tracks; this keeps the head gap normal to the recorded magnetic field over the whole usable head travel.

The storage capacity of a hard disk drive depends on:

- The track density on the platter.
- The bit density within a track.

These specifications vary greatly from one manufacturer to another. The IMI drive used in the Corvus system shown in Figures 12.10 through 12.12 stores 11 megabytes unformatted on two platters with three surfaces, a track density of 300 tracks per inch, and a recording density of 5,868 bits per inch. The Irwin drive shown in Figure 12.13 stores 12.3 megabytes on a single platter with two surfaces, a track density of 900 tracks per inch, and a recording density of 8,000 bits per inch.

12.7 HARD DISK CONTROLLERS

Hard disk controllers perform many of the same functions as the floppy disk controllers discussed earlier in this chapter, but have ad-

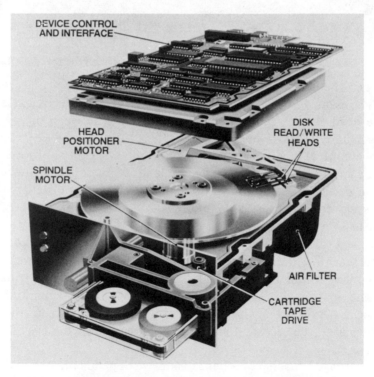

Figure 12.13.   Winchester disk drive with cartridge drive for streaming tape and device control with interface.

ditional functions related to the nature of the drive. For example, there is no head load function, because during operation the head is not in contact with the medium. On the other hand, an interlock prevents head movement while the drive is getting up to speed (and while it is slowing down after turn-off). Formatting requirements are somewhat more elaborate. Some interfaces allow sector sizes of 128 to 2,048 bytes or more, under control of the operating system.

Some hard disk controllers include provision for data transfers from the hard disk to a cartridge, open reel tape or floppy disk drive for backup: The Corvus system may use an optional video tape recorder; the Irwin drive has a built-in cartridge. The controller is housed in either the drive cabinet or separate enclosure; then there is an interface board which fits into the computer bus and attaches by cable to the controller. This interface board is generally a simple parallel or serial I/O port through which all command, status, and data bytes are transferred.

13
Disk Operating Systems

13.1 COMPONENTS OF A DISK OPERATING SYSTEM

A disk operating system (DOS) for a microcomputer performs many of the same functions of monitoring and data management as the operating systems for larger computers. However, single-user systems do not need multiprogramming or job control. Hence, the OS may be trimmed down to reside in a relatively small total amount of memory—16K or less—of which the OS occupies 5 to 6K. Only essential features are included. The 8080-based operating system called CP/M, sold by Digital Research, Inc., is typical, so we use it as our example. A minimal CP/M system has these components:

- A console command processor (CCP) identifies and executes commands given from the console.
- A file-management system (BDOS) keeps track of all records written to the disk and reuses disk space released by the deletion of records. This is the largest component.
- A logical I/O system (BIOS) provides names or number addresses for console, list, reader and punch for use by the CCP and BDOS and by application programs.
- A component that links driver routines for the physical I/O devices attached to the system to logical devices designated by the user or otherwise to standard default devices.